Structuralism and Since

Structuralism and Since

From Lévi-Strauss to Derrida

Edited, with an Introduction, by
JOHN STURROCK

Oxford New York Toronto Melbourne
OXFORD UNIVERSITY PRESS
1979

Oxford University Press, Walton Street, Oxford OX2 6DP

OXFORD LONDON GLASGOW
NEW YORK TORONTO MELBOURNE WELLINGTON
KUALA LUMPUR SINGAPORE JAKARTA HONG KONG TOKYO
DELHI BOMBAY CALCUTTA MADRAS KARACHI
IBADAN NAIROBI DAR ES SALAAM CAPE TOWN

ISBN 0 19 289105 7 *Paperback*
ISBN 0 19 215839 2 *Hardback*

*Typeset by Filmtype Services Ltd., Scarborough
and printed in Great Britain by
Cox & Wyman Ltd., Reading*

Contents

Introduction

In 1966 a much-reproduced cartoon appeared in a French literary periodical showing four of the thinkers with whom this book is concerned—Claude Lévi-Strauss, Roland Barthes, Michel Foucault, and Jacques Lacan—sitting on the ground beneath some tropical trees clad in the grass skirts and anklets of cartoon savages (the dandy of the group, Dr. Lacan, also wears a bow tie). The drawing needed no caption, but it has since gone under the title of 'Le déjeuner des structuralistes' or 'The structuralists' lunch party', even though the four figures are not eating but, more characteristically, holding forth.

The cartoon was not in the least unkind; the artist was not guying his subjects, merely acknowledging their arrival as a potent new force in French intellectual life. If they were got up as honorary South Sea islanders this was partly a tribute to the dominance at that time of Lévi-Strauss, an anthropologist who was best known for what he had written about the mental processes peculiar to so-called 'primitive' peoples, and partly a warning that many of the ideas which these four thinkers among them had to offer were exotic, and not easily to be assimilated to the prevailing intellectual climate in France. Frenchmen must be prepared to have their minds led into new, alien paths.

It would be foolish to read too much into the appearance of a single humorous drawing, however popular it proved. But the cartoonist had chosen his moment well. His immediate inspiration was the publication in Paris in 1966, within a few months of each other, of major works by Foucault and Lacan, *The Order of Things* and *Écrits*[1]—works of much difficulty and originality in their

---

[1] Works by the five writers in question are given their English titles throughout, where a translation exists; dates given are those of the works' original publication in French. Full information on books by the five writers is given in a bibliographical note at the end of each essay.

respective fields, the history of ideas and psychoanalysis. It seemed likely that a distinctive 'moment' had been reached in contemporary French thought, the first such moment since the triumph of Sartrean Existentialism in the years immediately after the end of the 1939–45 war. By the late 1960s existentialism as a creed was long defunct, even though some of its principal tenets had been absorbed into the mainstream of philosophical thought; and apart from Marxism, which remains a permanent option for any serious Parisian intellectual, there was no ideological movement to which it seemed possible to subscribe. 'Structuralism', in the persons of the four sages convened beneath the palm trees, seemed to offer just such an ideology. With the arrival of Foucault and Lacan to join the already respected Lévi-Strauss and Barthes, a new philosophy had become available—one of those crystallizations of which French intellectual history can provide numerous examples, whereby ideas hitherto dispersed and seemingly heterogeneous come together into a coherent whole.

Whether or not the ideas in question do form a coherent whole is a problem to which I shall address myself in this Introduction. I have already employed the word 'structuralism' within quotation marks, in order to distinguish the sociological phenomenon, of its rapid and wide popularity as a 'movement' in France and elsewhere, from the very undramatic set of principles which may be said to define structuralism on the philosophical plane. It has been many times said, in order to drive home this selfsame distinction, that structuralism is not a creed but a method: it is not possible to be a Structuralist in the way it was once possible to be an Existentialist—there are no structuralist night-clubs on the Left Bank, no structuralist clothes to wear or life-style to follow. It is simply a method of investigation, a particular way of approaching and, so structuralists maintain, of rationalizing the data belonging to a particular field of enquiry. It came into existence not suddenly in the 1960s in Paris but a good many years earlier and not in Paris. What happened in the 1960s in Paris was that this humdrum cognitive tool became glibly transformed into a slogan. 'Structuralism' was taken up and found to be exciting; an intellectual fashion was created and for a time all sense of proportion was lost. The fact that structuralism had thus been turned into a disreputable 'structuralism' was a source of some annoyance to a thinker such as Lévi-Strauss, a pure structuralist who clearly believed that his academic reputation would sink were he to be elevated against his will to the leadership of some new intellectual cult. Since then both structuralism and 'structuralism' have spread outside France, on a smaller scale and with less emotion, but producing none the less many of the same effects and confusions. Some have found structuralism a genuine revelation, able to reorient very fruitfully a whole approach to a particular field of study; others have found 'structuralism' a heady catchword, excellent for flaunting at opponents or as a badge of membership in an arcane brotherhood.

The aim of the present book is to elucidate, without fear or favour, the work of five French thinkers commonly associated with 'structuralism'; and the aim of my preliminary remarks here must be to determine what the common ground is between the five of them which justifies their appearance together in the one book. The title of the cartoon I have described, 'The structuralists' lunch party', is to some extent unfortunate. It implies a degree of convergence in the thinking of the four figures represented there which could never be proved from their writings. Some of these four 'structuralists' are more structuralist than others.

At one extreme, and it is for this reason that the essay on him is the first in the book, stands Lévi-Strauss, who has chosen to identify his life's work absolutely with the method of investigation on which it has been founded. He flies his structuralist colours in the titles of some of his books: *The Elementary Structures of Kinship* (1949), or the two volumes of *Structural Anthropology* (1958 and 1973). His commitment to structuralism is straightforward and total. It is the method by which he believes he has made more intelligible than ever before the empirical data on the institutions of kinship, totemism, and myth. Indeed, he passes beyond mere explanation of these data to the identification of what he takes to be specific, universal properties of the human mind itself. In the present company, Lévi-Strauss stands on his own for his consistency of method, his rationalism, and the directness with which he communicates his findings and arguments to his readers.

None of the other four thinkers here would be at all happy to be labelled a 'structuralist', which each would see as a gross violation of his freedom of thought. Barthes is a great eclectic so far as the methods he has pursued in his studies of literature go, and an extreme believer in the need constantly to move on from one theoretical position to another; at various times he has adopted methods clearly learnt from the other subjects of this book. Foucault has protested publicly at being thought a 'structuralist' and for reasons very like those Barthes would use: he is another who wishes not to occupy a determinate position along the ideological or intellectual spectrum, but to remain freely mobile, turning up now in this part of the landscape, now in that, in order to question various of the historical and contemporary forms of knowledge and power without being himself submitted to questioning. To the query 'Where does Foucault stand?' there is no easy answer. Lacan is a man of famously arrogant independence who prefers others to follow and be influenced by him, rather than to appear himself to be following or even associating with others. His great desire is to re-present Freud in a country that has failed more signally than most to come to terms with Freudian ideas; there is no evidence that he has paid any heed to the work of his contemporaries among French thinkers. Derrida, finally, came to prominence at a later date than the other thinkers considered here (by 1966 he had published no full-length book of his own; though in the following year he published no less than three), and as a result has been associated less with 'structuralism'. Indeed, he has become, willingly or not, the undisputed inspiration of that follow-up to it now known as 'post-structuralism', largely because an important part of his work has been to read carefully the theoretical work of his contemporaries and expose certain of their unexamined assumptions. Derrida, moreover, like Barthes and Foucault, is a bitter opponent of transcendent systems of thought which purport to offer their adherents positions of dominance from which they can look down in detachment and judge others accordingly. He too is always in movement across the intellectual landscape.

Here is one way, then, of separating the five thinkers into two opposed categories. Lévi-Strauss and Lacan are both universalists, both are concerned with the operations performed by the human mind in general, not just with the workings of particular minds at particular times. Lévi-Strauss claims to have located, behind a diversity of empirical facts, a universal mental structure. Lacan, as a psychoanalyst concerned with theory, not simply with particular experiences in the consulting room or the therapy of individual patients, would also claim to be legislating for the functioning of the human psyche in general. By contrast, Barthes, Foucault, and Derrida appear as relativists, preoccupied with the historical dimension of thought, its evolution through time, and its implications for given societies. They forbear to transcend their subject-matter as Lévi-Strauss and Lacan do, to construct an equivalent of the latters' meta-anthropology and meta-psychology.

I use this as one example of how these five thinkers can be compared and classified; in other perspectives they would fall, naturally, into other categories. All manner of contrasts and comparisons might be made between them, but to make these would be to stress the divergence of their ideas instead of their convergence. At some points they coincide, at others they do not. It would be an extremely complex task to establish all the degrees of affinity between five men working in quite different areas of research; and I do not think it would be worth undertaking since it would prove nothing very much. This does not mean, however, that this particular constellation of thinkers is fortuitous, to be justified by no argument stronger than the topical one, that they came on the scene more or less simultaneously. There are many points of intersection in their work, and the five essays that follow constantly reinforce one another. These 'structuralists' may lack a common programme but they do not lack a common ancestry. It is principally in the genealogy of their ideas that one should look for evidence of their kinship.

This common ancestry is very much a matter of vocabulary: a certain terminology recurs in their work, and recurs, inevitably, in any elucidation of that work by others. It is a terminology familiar enough in France but less so elsewhere, and it bears out a remark made by Barthes in his *Critical Essays* (1964), that 'It is probably in the serious recourse to the lexicon of signification . . . that we must finally see the spoken sign of structuralism.' This may not have the expected form or assurance of a definition, but it may be taken as one. What Barthes is saying is that a true ('serious') structuralist is to be recognized by the use he makes of a number of technical terms, taken over, as it happens, from structural linguistics. One of these terms he has contrived, slyly, to incorporate in his own definition, as an instant declaration of his loyalties. The term is *sign*, which is central to the 'lexicon of signification'.

This lexicon derives from the extraordinarily innovative work of the Swiss linguist Ferdinand de Saussure (1857–1913), whose theoretical work on natural or human language in the early years of the present century lies behind all of modern structuralism. Saussure has acquired far less esteem and influence in Anglo-Saxon countries than he has in France, where he is one of the great father-figures of the contemporary mind. All five of our thinkers depend fundamentally on his insights into language, and in particular into the nature of the basic unit of any language, the linguistic sign. We need not attempt here to give a definition of the sign, which is exceedingly difficult. We can say instead that any word in a language is a sign, and that language functions as a system of signs.

Saussure analysed the sign into its two components: a sound or acoustic component which he called the *signifier* (*signifiant* in French), and a mental or conceptual component which he called the *signified* (*signifié*). In this analysis, be it noted, things themselves, for which linguistic signs can be asked to stand when we want to refer to the world around us, are ignored. The signified is not a thing but the notion of a thing, what comes into the mind of the speaker or hearer when the appropriate signifier is uttered. The signifier thus constitutes the material aspect of language: in the case of the spoken language a signifier is any meaningful sound which is uttered or heard, in the case of the written language it is a meaningful mark inscribed on the page. The signified is the mental aspect of language which we often deem to be immaterial, even though it is certain that within the brain a signified is also a neural event. Signifiers and signifieds can be separated in this way only by the theorist of language; in practice they are inseparable. A truly meaningless sound is not a signifier because it does not signify—there can be no signifier without a signified;[2] correspondingly, no concept can be said to exist unless it has found expression, that is to say been materialized, either inwardly as a thought or outwardly in speech—there can be no signified without a signifier.

[2] One must be careful here because it is simple to invent 'nonsense' signifiers; these, however, signify 'meaninglessness', and so have a valid signified after all.

These three terms, *sign* and its two components, together make up the 'lexicon of signification' to which Barthes alludes and which he sees as sufficient proof of a particular writer's affiliation to structuralism. The distinction between signifier and signified is one that requires to be kept in mind when reading the five essays in this book, none of which would entirely make sense without it. It is a distinction which can also be applied in situations other than the analysis of the constituent signs of natural language. We have experience in our daily lives of a great many signs that are not verbal ones: of pictures and diagrams, for instance. And it is a fact that any object whatsoever, be it natural or artificial, can become a sign provided that it is employed to communicate a message, i.e. to *signify*. The flower that grows only to blush unseen can never be a sign since there is no one present to turn it into one. But within a culture flowers can be and are used as signs: when they are made into a wreath and sent to a funeral, for example. In this instance, the wreath is the signifier whose signified is, let us say, 'condol-ence'. (There can be no precise signified for a wreath because the language of flowers is too loose, at any rate in our culture; but equally there can be no wreath without a significance of some kind.)

The nature of the message conveyed by signs such as wreaths of flowers is one determined by the culture in which the sender and recipient live. Flowers have no *natural* significance, only a cultural or conventional one. (It is Lévi-Strauss above all who has driven home the lesson that we should never confuse the natural with the cultural when to do so is to fail to remark what is specifically human.) When they are employed as signs they enter into what is often referred to as a *code*, a channel of communication linking the two parties to any such cultural transaction. It is worth pointing out that in just the same way groups of words can themselves form a single sign: groups of signs can, that is to say, form one sign. They do so, indeed, in the quotation I have given from Barthes, where the 'lexicon of signification', consisting of three separate signs, is itself used as a sign; as such it conveys, to whomever is equipped to interpret it, the message 'I am a structuralist'. The study of signs in general, and of the operation of the vast number of codes in any culture which enable us to interpret these signs satisfactorily, is now practised under the name of semiology in France and other

European countries, and of semiotics in the United States.[3] It was Saussure, again, who first called for the institution of such a general science of signs.

He also introduced two other pairs of contrasted terms which are important to any understanding of the style of thought we are faced with. In the study of language he distinguished first of all between what he called *langue* and *parole*, or 'language' and 'speech'. *Language* is the theoretical system or structure of a language, the corpus of linguistic rules which speakers of that language must obey if they are to communicate; *speech* is the actual day-to-day use made of that system by individual speakers. This distinction can usefully be compared to the rather better-known one popularized more recently by the American grammarian Noam Chomsky, who distinguishes between our linguistic *competence* and our linguistic *performance*, meaning respectively the theory of language we appear to be able to carry constantly in our heads and the practical applications we make of it. For Saussure the linguist's proper job was to study not speech but language, because it was only by doing so that he could grasp the principles on which language functions in practice. This same important distinction emerges, in the work examined in this book, as one between *structure* and *event*, that is to say between abstract systems of rules and the concrete, individual happenings produced within that system. The relation between one and the other, and the question of which should take precedence—do structures precede events, or events structures?—has been much debated.

A second and, for my purposes here, final Saussurian distinction is that between the *synchronic* and the *diachronic* axes of investigation. It is permissible to study language—to take Saussure's own subject—along two radically different axes: as a system functioning at a given moment in time, or as an institution which has evolved through time. Saussure himself advocated the synchronic study of language, by contrast with the diachronic studies of the linguists who were his predecessors in the nineteenth century.

---

[3] Interestingly, this pair of alternative terms themselves form a simple code. If I say 'I am a semiologist' I declare my loyalty to the Saussurian or European model of sign study; if, on the other hand, I say 'I am a semiotician', then I ally myself with the North American model, inspired by the great pragmatist philosopher C. S. Peirce.

They had been preoccupied by the history of particular languages, by etymologies, phonetic change, and the like, and had never stopped to try and work out the total structure of a language, freezing it at a set moment of its evolution the easier to comprehend the principles on which it functioned.

Synchronic, or structural, linguistics thus introduced a revolutionary shift in perspective. It would have recognized that a total study of language must combine both perspectives, but it was prepared to ignore the diachronic perspective in order to set linguistics on a sounder, more productive footing. Structuralism as a whole is necessarily synchronic; it is concerned to study particular systems or structures under artificial and ahistorical conditions, neglecting the systems or structures out of which they have emerged in the hope of explaining their present functioning. This is why, in France especially, structuralism has often found itself at odds with Marxism, for which any such denial of history is unthinkable. Marxism, that supremely historicist interpretation of the social reality, is diachronic; it could never reach an accommodation with a pure structuralism.

Another influence on structuralism to be traced to Saussure's linguistics is not a matter of vocabulary, but is the most profound—and also the most elusive—of all. A crucial premise of Saussure's theory of language is that the linguistic sign is 'arbitrary'. It is so in two ways: the signifier is arbitrary inasmuch as there is no natural, only a conventional, link between it and the thing it signifies (not the signified in this case). There is no property common to all trees, for instance, which makes it logical or necessary that we should refer to them as 'trees'. That is what we, as anglophone persons, call them by agreement among ourselves; the French choose differently, they refer to them as *'arbres'*. But language is arbitrary at the level of the signified also, for each native language divides up in different ways the total field of what may be expressed in words, as one soon finds out in the act of translating from one language to another. One language has concepts that are absent from another. The example which linguists like to give of such arbitrariness is that of colour terms, which vary greatly from one language to another, even though the colours themselves form a continuum and, being determined naturally by their wave frequency, are universal.

The extremely important consequence which Saussure draws from this twofold arbitrariness is that language is a system not of fixed, unalterable essences but of labile forms. It is a system of relations between its constituent units, and those units are themselves constituted by the differences that mark them off from other, related units. They cannot be said to have any existence within themselves, they are dependent for their identity on their fellows. It is the place which a particular unit, be it phonetic or semantic, occupies in the linguistic system which alone determines its value. Those values shift because there is nothing to hold them steady; the system is fundamentally arbitrary in respect of nature and what is arbitrary may be changed.

'Language is a form and not a substance' was Saussure's famous summation of this quite fundamental insight, an insight without which none of the work done by Lévi-Strauss, Barthes, and the others would have been feasible. Structuralism holds to this vital assumption, that it studies relations between mutually conditioned elements of a system and not between self-contained essences. It is easiest once more to instantiate this from linguistics. There is nothing essential or self-contained about a given word; the word 'rock', let us take. That occupies a certain space, both phonetically and semantically. Phonetically it can only be defined by establishing what the limits of that space are: where the boundaries lie if it crosses which it changes from being the word 'rock' to being a different sign of the language—'ruck', for instance, or 'wreck', which abut on it acoustically. Semantically, we can only delimit the meaning of the signifier 'rock' by differentiating it from other signs which abut on it semantically, such as 'stone', 'boulder', 'cliff'.

In short, without difference there can be no meaning. A one-term language is an impossibility because its single term could be applied to everything and differentiate nothing; it requires at least one other term to give it definition. It would be possible, if rudimentary, to differentiate the entire contents of the universe by means of a two-term code or language, as being either *bing* or *bong* perhaps. But without the introduction of that small phonetic difference, between the two vowel sounds, we can have no viable language at all.

This brief lesson in structural linguistics is an essential background to all five essays in this book. The implications of Saussure's work on language are seen at their clearest in the work of Lévi-Strauss, who has declared Saussure to be one of the two truly formative influences in his intellectual life (the other being a sixteenth-century French Protestant missionary to Brazil, who produced the first recognizably modern ethnographic account of an indigenous population). Lévi-Strauss has studied anthropological phenomena as if they were languages (failing, according to Dan Sperber, to recognize in so doing that he was using the term 'language' metaphorically). He has studied them, that is, as systems: the systems of kinship, of totemism, of myth. He has attended to the relations between the different units of each system and found how the function of what might at first sight appear to be the same unit varies with the relations it enters into with other units. This is most striking when it comes to the interpretation of symbolic elements in a myth, since we many of us lean to the belief that symbols are fixed quantities, susceptible wherever they occur of a single interpretation. Lévi-Strauss shows otherwise: that their meaning at each recurrence is fixed by the place they occupy within the economy of that particular myth.

This is to interpret myths from within, to allow the system itself as it were to dictate the meaning to you; and it is easy to see from this how structuralism can be extended to the study of literature or other bodies of writing. It practises, first and foremost, an 'immanent' type of criticism, refusing to look outside the text or group of texts with which it is engaged in order to seek an explanation of their structure. The value of a character in a play, for example, is estimated by the same procedure as one might use to estimate the value of a word in a given language, by comparison not with the world outside the play but with the economy of the play itself, with the other characters it contains. The differences between characters are the clue to their dramatic significance; the fond, dutiful Cordelia would lack all definition were she an only child, deprived of the comparisons available to readers of *Lear* in the characters of Goneril and Regan.

Only a fanatical structuralist would argue that to uncover the system of a literary work by means such as these is the whole of literary criticism, and that the structuralist holds the ultimate key to literary understanding. A moderate structuralism is true to its own tenets, and admits that a structuralist interpretation is defined by the differences that exist between it and other interpretations. The 'immanent' reading of a text of which I have spoken is defined by contrasting it with the many forms of 'transcendent' reading open to a critic: to 'biographical' readings, say, whereby the critic explains what transpires in a book or play in terms of events known to have taken place in the author's life. Structuralism is opposed to criticism of that kind, I believe rightly; but it has never proposed to suppress it.

From all I have been saying it will be apparent that the question of language is absolutely at the forefront of the style of thought we are concerned with. In this, contemporary French thought echoes what has been happening in Anglo-American philosophy in the past twenty years, where both the practical and theoretical aspects of language have come to dominate. This is because language is no longer the simple, transparent medium of thought it was once accepted as being. We prefer now to equate language with thought; and instead of looking through it, at reality, we look at it, in an attempt to understand how we first of all acquire it and then use it.

Language plays a central part in the thought of Barthes, Foucault, Derrida, and Lacan, as it does in the anthropology of Lévi-Strauss. All of them, it could be said, are obsessed by it. They are obsessed by the institutional nature of language, and by its infinite productivity. It is not something we each bring with us into the world at birth, but an institution into which we are gradually initiated in childhood as the most fundamental element of all in our socialization. Language can thus be described as impersonal, it exceeds us as individuals. Any use of language to communicate with others (or even with ourselves) involves us inevitably in the surrender of a portion at least of our uniqueness, since if our language also were unique no one would be able to understand it. In the terms favoured by Lacan, some of our libido must be surrendered to the system: we must pass from the private, if also delusive order of what he calls the Imaginary, to the social order of the Symbolic. Our individuality is correspondingly reduced.

A more considerable loss of individuality is incurred when the Symbolic order to which we yield is not the primary one, of language as such, but the secondary one of literature, or of discourse in general, where further, frequently severe, restrictions by way of conventions are placed on us to prevent us using language with the freedom we might like. Now it is the Symbolic order in which structuralism is interested, because that order is the system in which we ourselves can never be more than 'events'. In consequence structuralism has come to stand for a way of thinking opposed to individualism, or even to humanism, for intentional human agency is given a reduced role in its interpretations of culture. Much has been written of 'the disappearance of the subject' under the structuralist dispensation, meaning that structuralism has carried its strong bias against essentialism so far as somehow to deny the existence of human beings altogether, and to see the individual as nothing better than an unstable, replaceable form within a soulless system.

Certainly there is much hostility to all philosophies of individualism in these thinkers' writings. They all, some more than others, subscribe to the strongly anti-bourgeois sentiments traditional among French intellectuals, for whom the bourgeois is a corrupt and thus typical member of the middle classes who has managed to disguise his own insatiable greed for money and power as a noble philosophy of liberal self-development. Thus there is a political slant to the ideas of such as Foucault and Barthes; but that is by no means the end of it. Their war on what we might call ego philosophies goes deeper than that. Its theoretical underpinning comes out very well in the work of Lacan. He has done much to persuade us to abandon whatever belief we cling to in the autonomy of the ego, not as an agent in society but as an agent controlling our own words and actions. In Lacan's view, Freud's discoveries about the constitution of the human psyche were so shocking that they were subsequently repressed, as undesirable. Lacan, after Freud, dwells on the function of the Id, those disruptive impulses of the subconscious which refuse all authority and stability to the Ego. The Ego, in Lacan's scheme, belongs to the Symbolic order, it is a false construct which we are induced to make after our earliest experiences as an infant of seeing ourselves reflected in mirrors and so assuming that we possess a permanent and unchanging kernel of identity.

Derrida's patient, intricate campaign to destroy the privilege accorded in western cultures to speech over writing, as twin modes of language use, has broadly similar effects, since writing is that mode of language use in which the human individual is not present to authenticate it. A written text is customarily attributed to an individual author, but it does not need to be: there are collective texts, and many anonymous ones which we have no right to deduce are the work of unknown individuals. Even in the standard case, where a text *is* attributed to a single, named individual, Derrida's argument is that the text has in fact been set free from the individual who produced it, who may very well be dead. An author can have no special authority over what he has written and then published, because he has committed it both to strangers and to the future. The meanings it will henceforth yield need not coincide with those he believed he had invested in it: they will depend on who reads it and in what circumstances. The circuit of the communication of meaning is all the less sure for no longer being immediate, as it is when meanings pass from speaker to hearer, i.e. from one physical presence to another.

Again, Derrida's celebrated 'deconstructions' of the philosophical and other writings he has analysed, in which he brings to light the internal contradictions in seemingly perfectly coherent systems of thought, constitute a powerful attack on ordinary notions of authorship, identity, and selfhood, since they are a demonstration that, even when it is being used most consciously, language has powers we cannot control. Derrida himself exploits the alarming 'productivity' of language to destabilize existing philosophical systems.

Foucault has found fame above all by challenging the power that has been exercised by those in intellectual authority in every society and at all times, to lay down what may or may not be said. Power is used to subdue desire: in Freudian terms the Superego works to hold down the Id. But Foucault is on the side of the free play of desire, of those social deviants of one sort or another who have been cast on to the margins of society and treated as alien or sick. Barthes glories in what he calls the 'cacography' (this being the written version of an aural cacophony) which the nature of language makes possible; those contradictory thoughts we are all of us capable of and which make it hard indeed to defend the notion that deep within us there is some utterly consistent essence of which our public behaviour is the unique expression.

So there is a common ideology at work here: of dissolution, of disbelief in the ego. The self, in the traditional sense, would appear to such as Foucault as a 'theological' notion, a false transcendence. All these thinkers are against authority, and against metaphysics. They do not wish to transcend what they see, in pursuit of some hidden, ultimate meaning which would 'explain' everything; they do not believe that everything can be explained. Nor do they hold with teleological interpretations of history. They are against the singular and for the plural, preferring whole galaxies of meanings to emerge from a limited set of phenomena to the notion that it must hold one, unifying, dominant meaning. They believe, where meaning is concerned, in 'dissemination' (the word is Derrida's).

To revert for a moment to the linguistic plane: what these five thinkers have very influentially done is to advance the claims of the signifier above those of the signified. The signifier is what we can be sure of, it is material; the signified is an open question. The same signifier is sure to have different signifieds for two different people, occupying a differently defined semantic space because of the dissimilarity of individual experience; again, the same signifier will have different signifieds for the same person at different times, since the configuration of our semantic space is never stable. Structuralism invites us to delight in the plurality of meaning this opens up, to reject the authoritarian or unequivocal interpretation of signs. Lévi-Strauss presents his own interpretations of Amerindian myths as *possible* interpretations and leaves the way open for alternative ones to follow; he is demonstrating a method, not seeking to establish some final truth. Meanings may and should coexist, there is no call for one to be exalted at the expense of others. The more meaning there is in our world the better: or so would say the subjects of this book.

I have left until last another linguistic matter: the problem of the prose style in which those subjects have chosen to present their case to the world. It is a style in most cases of some, or even extreme difficulty. Lévi-Strauss is at times a complex writer but never an altogether obscure one: his writing is abstract and makes stiff demands on our intelligence if we are to keep up with it. Barthes I do not myself find an obscure writer though there are others who do claim to find him so. He is an ambitious writer in terms of the concepts he is dealing with and there are paragraphs in his books which may well be more ambiguous than he intended them to be, as well as pairs of terms the distinction between which is exceedingly elusive. Both Foucault and Derrida represent a greater degree of difficulty than Barthes, although both are capable of directness (there is a journalistic side to Foucault which makes him at rare moments perfectly accessible). Lacan, however, is something of a legendary case. The French in which he writes is of high idiosyncrasy, its syntax being deliberately contrived in order to exemplify rather than to explicate the linguistic operations of the unconscious. Lacan's language can reduce the most co-operative reader to despair; nor is it possible to translate it satisfactorily because it is full of word play and allusion, being required by Lacan to prove that the unconscious works with signifiers not signifieds to construct the verbal chain.

Writings as hard to grasp as those of Lacan, and to a lesser degree those of Derrida, Foucault, and Barthes, have given 'structuralism' a bad name in some quarters. They have inspired a high level of intolerance among those who insist that clarity of exposition is a prerequisite in any thinker. Intelligent if hasty commentators have concluded that Lacan is unintelligible and that his followers therefore can be no more than willing stooges. One may wish that Lacan were an easier writer to understand—I wish so myself; but it is peculiarly sterile to scoff at him as if his work were worthless. It makes better sense to ponder the reasons why he writes in the style he does.

It is not that he has aimed at clarity of exposition and failed, any more than Barthes, Derrida, or Foucault has done. They simply do not agree that clarity is the universal virtue or imperative their critics claim it to be. They write, it should be remembered, in a country where clarity (*la clarté*) has been regarded as a national virtue, the mark (or *sign*) of a truly French mind. In the French educational world it has been a fetish, a fine example of a cultural value masquerading as a natural one. It was one of Barthes's earlier acts to try and undermine the authority of such an idea. He argued that *la clarté* was adopted as a national virtue for the unworthiest of reasons: the ascendant bourgeoisie had grasped that it was a virtue appropriate to any class anxious to impose its will on those beneath it in the social hierarchy, because it was the virtue appropriate to the discourse of persuasion and autocracy.

Writers like these, then, know exactly what they are doing when they offend so egregiously against the canon. They are demonstrating that there is far more to language than lucidity. Lucidity gives us the illusion that we have language firmly under our thumb, that we are making it do exactly what we want. Lacan and the others (I except Lévi-Strauss from this) would remove that illusion. They would rather show what a large degree of autonomy language enjoys, and that there is infinitely more to be said on every topic than will ever be said by those who believe that anything worth saying must be said unambiguously. Ambiguity itself becomes a virtue if one shares in what is basically a post-Freudian view of language and its resources. If we read Lacan only with extreme difficulty, Lacan would say that was good—that in struggling to explain to ourselves what he is getting at we shall de-inhibit our own minds. The relationship between writer and reader becomes more democratic when the writer no longer hands down to us from on high his firm doctrine, in all its illusory simplicity, but sets us to work picking our way through his ambiguities, gathering meanings as we go. These are not seminal but 'disseminal' works.

All five of the thinkers in this book are also *writers*. They are self-conscious about the form of what they write, and knowledgeable about the devices and effects of rhetoric. Only the work of Lévi-Strauss can readily be assigned to a traditional academic discipline; the others might claim to belong to literature as much as to criticism, or history, or psychoanalysis, or philosophy. Indeed, it is distinctions such as these, between creative writing and criticism with Barthes, or between poetry and psychoanalytical writing in Lacan's case, or between literature and philosophy in Foucault and Derrida, that they are committed to abolishing. Their style is part of the attempt. They refuse to be imprisoned within the far narrower stylistic bounds of orthodox academic discourse. The extravagance of their style should be an attraction to us, not an impediment. It is a calculated challenge to our expectations, as readers of history, philosophy, literary criticism, or whatever we choose to call it, which there is both pleasure and intellectual reward in trying to meet.

JOHN STURROCK

April 1979

Claude Lévi-Strauss

DAN SPERBER

No anthropologist has ever gained greater fame than Claude Lévi-Strauss, yet few have been more abstruse. In his case, both the fame and the abstruseness spring from partly common causes: the scale of his intellectual enterprise, its reflexive dimension, and the poetic, often ambiguous, quality of his thought and his style of writing.

Most anthropologists devote themselves to the meticulous description of a single people; they limit their theoretical ambitions to improving classifications or to short- or middle-range generalizations about 'bridewealth' in Africa, or 'big-manship' in Melanesia. If challenged to express views about features characteristic of the human species as a whole, they are likely to assert that *Homo sapiens* is a viviparous biped animal that speaks and is endowed with superior learning abilities. Such theorizing does not attract mass audiences. As Edmund Leach has pointed out in connection with Malinowski and Frazer, sex and metaphysics have been the anthropologists' paths to popularity.

This theoretical timidity is not wholly unjustified. Speculating about 'human nature' (to use the old phrase) is no easy matter, and it is unclear whether anthropologists are any better equipped for it than, say, experimental psychologists. Indeed their main contribution has been one of dissuasion, by showing that, most of the time, what were taken to be natural phenomena were in fact cultural ones. Many anthropologists have even claimed that there is no such thing as a human nature, not realizing that they were thereby denying the very existence of a subject-matter for anthropology.

Lévi-Strauss's innovation was to take hold of this dilemma by both horns: rather than opposing human nature to cultural variety as two incompatible notions, he has attempted to show that the first lies behind the second as a unified, abstract structure governing concrete, observable variations. This principle is not new. It was taken for granted by classical philosophers of human nature. But they did not have to face the challenge of modern ethnographical knowledge. Lévi-Strauss set himself the task of renovating this principle, while at the same time meeting the new challenge, by attempting simultaneously to make better sense of cultural peculiarities and to establish the intellectual unity of mankind. The task is truly a difficult one, calling for scientific creativity in a domain where scientific progress has hitherto been mostly destructive—of misconceptions. It seems unavoidable that Lévi-Strauss should introduce unconventional notions, maintain paradoxical hypotheses, appeal to vague intuitions, and experiment with sketchy models.

An important part of Lévi-Strauss's work is of a reflexive nature. In *Tristes tropiques* (1955), his philosophical autobiography, in his *Conversations* with Georges Charbonnier (1961), in about half the essays in *Structural Anthropology* (1958) and *Anthropologie structurale deux* (1973), and in long passages in his other works, Lévi-Strauss considers the fate of anthropology and his own fate, advocates his 'structural method', illustrating it with *ad hoc* examples, assesses the potential contribution of 'structuralism' to other fields of inquiry, and points out its philosophical implications.

Understandably, these self-interpretative writings have been more widely read and discussed than those which deal directly with anthropological issues. Much praise and criticism have been directed at Lévi-Strauss's expositions of structuralism with few stopping to ask themselves whether these give an adequate account of his actual practice. That he might be wrong about the human species in general is obvious; that he might be wrong about himself is usually not even considered. I shall maintain that in some important respects Lévi-Strauss is right about human nature and possibly misleading about his own work.

Take a marginal but characteristic instance: he asserts that all myths can be reduced to a canonical formula:

$$Fx \ (a) : Fy \ (b) : : Fx \ (b) : Fa^{-1} \ (y)$$

In *Structural Anthropology* he explains this formula in one short paragraph. In *From Honey to Ashes*, he cites it again and adds: 'It was necessary to quote it at least once more as proof of the fact that

I have never ceased to be guided by it.' Should a chemist or a generative linguist make a similar claim, he would be expected to elaborate upon his formula beyond any risk of vagueness or ambiguity. Lévi-Strauss does nothing of the kind. He does not give a single step-by-step example of its use, he does not even mention his formula anywhere else in his work. Most commentators have wisely pretended that it does not exist.

There is no reason to doubt Lévi-Strauss's good faith; yet what on earth *is* he asserting? The answer is easy enough once one realizes that he tends to lump together his investigative strategy, his methodology, and his theory: the individual paths he has happened to follow, the shared ground-rules of scholarship, and the general empirical assumptions he has arrived at. When he claims that he has 'never ceased to be guided' by his formula, it is rather like a transcendental meditator claiming to be guided by his mantra ('only those who practise [structural analysis] know through intimate experience the sentiment of plenitude this produces, by which the mind feels in true communion with the body'—*L'Homme nu*). It is an autobiographical fact which there is little reason either to question or to emulate.

Similarly when, in *Tristes tropiques*, Lévi-Strauss talks of geology, Marxism, and psychoanalysis as his 'three mistresses' ('three sources of inspiration' in the most recent English translation), he is describing how his ideas took shape, not what they are. In more conventional thinkers, there may be a quite straightforward relation between the two, but not with Lévi-Strauss, who has an extraordinary ability to perceive and exploit the most indirect relationships. Thus in his case direct inspiration may have been less decisive than a realization of the potential fruitfulness of developing views symmetrically opposed to those of the then influential French philosopher, Henri Bergson, by stressing discontinuity rather than continuity, intellect rather than emotion.

Lévi-Strauss is not simply a scholar; he is also an artist. His choice of topics, examples, references, and points of comparison shows a highly unconventional eclecticism. The indexes to his books read like surrealist inventories, and the relation which the illustrations bear to his text is often only to be guessed at. The titles and organization of the chapters in his books on myth suggest a musical composition rather than a work of scholarship, with an 'overture' and a 'finale', and 'sonata', 'fugue', 'cantata', 'symphony', 'variations', etc., along the way.

Even more noticeably, Lévi-Strauss's use of figures of speech is truly original (and sometimes disconcerting). With most writers, concrete metaphors, allegories, or examples tend to be used to illustrate or express more abstract ideas, but Lévi-Strauss's imagination often works the other way round. He has a special taste for abstract, formal figures of speech (which his readers too often confuse with actual abstraction or formalism).

One of his favourite figures is a fairly rare form of 'abstract for concrete' substitution, or synecdoche, whereby a quality is used as an equivalent for the person or thing which possesses it: a calabash is referred to as a 'container', the beverage in it as the 'contained'. A moccasin is a 'cultural object', grass a 'natural object'. Less trivially, bone is referred to as 'the reverse of food', a thorn bush as 'nature hostile to man', a moccasin again as 'anti-land', and so on. When, on a rare occasion, Lévi-Strauss uses a concrete, everyday metaphor, and compares a system of symbolic classification to 'a utensil with crossed metal blades which is used for cutting potatoes into slices or chips', he immediately re-describes the utensil in wholly abstract terms: 'A "preconceived" grid is applied to all the empirical situations with which it has sufficient affinities for the elements obtained always to preserve certain general properties' (*The Savage Mind*).

These abstract synecdoches become the instruments of a second favourite figure of speech: antithesis. A container is contrasted with a contained, a cultural object with a natural one, etc. The more elaborate abstract synecdoches enable the antithesis to be further developed into a chiasmus, or 'symmetrical inversion' in Lévi-Strauss's terms. Here is an excellent specimen of the kind (he is talking about Western, more specifically French, cultural images of domestic animals): 'If birds are *metaphorical human beings* and dogs *metonymical human beings*, cattle may be thought of as *metonymical inhuman beings* and racehorses as *metaphorical inhuman beings*' (ibid.).

These peculiar figures of speech are used by Lévi-Strauss at two levels: in analysing cultural categories (as in the examples above), or in reflecting on anthropological notions. I shall argue later that at the first level this can often be illuminating, but at the second, reflexive, level, it tends to be a source of confusion. Take a typical instance; Lévi-Strauss claims we should regard

> marriage regulations and kinship systems as a kind of language, a set of processes permitting the establishment, between individuals and groups, of a certain type of communication. That the mediating factor, in this case, should be the *women of the group*, who are *circulated* between clans, lineages, or families, in place of the *words of the group*, which are *circulated* between individuals, does not at all change the fact that the essential aspect of the phenomenon is identical in both cases.
>
> (*Structural Anthropology*)

How is this striking conclusion arrived at? First, by way of two abstract synecdoches: marriage regulations and kinship systems are thereby reduced to the circulation of women, and spoken language to the circulation of words. Second, by a 'species for genus' synecdoche, all kinds of circulation are equated with one special form of it, namely communication. Third, by another similar synecdoche, communication is equated with one of its special forms: language (not spoken language here, but language as a general, abstract category).

Each of these steps is open to objection. Marriage and kinship involve much more than the circulation of women: they involve the organization of corporate groups, the transmission of rights, property, and knowledge, of conventional attitudes and expectations, the circulation of various kinds of goods, and so on. But Lévi-Strauss has devoted a whole book (*The Elementary Structures of Kinship*) to arguing that the circulation of women is 'the central aspect' of kinship.

On the other hand, the innocent-looking assertion that the circulation of words is the essential aspect of spoken language is smuggled in. In Saussurian terms, the way in which words circulate is an aspect of *parole* and not of *langue*; or in Chomskyan terms, of linguistic performance not of competence. The structure of spoken language determines not who says what to whom, but what can be said at all in a given tongue, irrespective of who the interlocutors are. A spoken language is a *code* which determines what messages are available for (among other possible uses) circulation in the social network(s) to which the speakers belong. By contradistinction, a marriage system is a *network*, whose structure determines which channels between social groups are open to the 'circulation of women'. Women are made available for (among other destinations) circulation along these channels not by any kind of code, but through biological reproduction. So, even if one accepts the notion that both spoken language and kinship are communication systems, the 'essential aspect' of one is a code and of the other a network—two very different kinds of structure.

In any case, to equate circulation with communication is also objectionable. If I circulate some words to you, we do indeed communicate: I had some information that you did not have, and now we share it. On the other hand, if I have a cow and I give it to you, this is unquestionably circulation, but not communication: at the end of such a process, we need have no more in common than we had at the start.

Nor should it be taken for granted that 'a set of processes permitting the establishment, between individuals and groups, of a certain type of communication' is necessarily 'a kind of language'. Information can be transmitted in two ways: either by coding it in a shared language or by drawing attention to it, by displaying it. For instance, if I am told to go away, I can say 'I refuse to go' or I can behave in such a way as to make it clear that I refuse to go; either way I succeed in transmitting the information. Most human communication involves a mixture of these two forms. Now if we accept, for the sake of argument, Lévi-Strauss's notion that women are the messages communicated in a kinship system, surely these messages consist of displayed rather than coded information, and are not in any sense 'linguistic'.

Thus the assertion that a kinship system is a language can only be analysed as a complex metaphor based on questionable synecdoches. But the greater part of Lévi-Strauss's work is more modest, more painstaking, and much more relevant to anthropological understanding, even though his style remains a baroque combination of order and fantasy.

Lévi-Strauss's work falls into three groups, if we leave aside the miscellaneous papers collected in *Structural Anthropology* and *Anthropologie structurale deux*: First, his doctoral dissertation, *The Elementary Structures of Kinship*, published in 1949, revised in 1967, and published in English in 1969, which has been a source of much controversy. Second, two books, *Totemism* and *The Savage Mind* (both 1962), on the classificatory activities of the human mind, the theme most central to all his work. Third, the four volumes of his *Introduction to a Science of Mythology* (in French, more elegantly, *Mythologiques*): *The Raw and the Cooked* (1964), *From Honey to Ashes* (1967), *The Origin of Table Manners* (1968), and *L'Homme nu* (1971).

Rather than try to summarize the general ideas contained in these works, I shall present selected examples and issues from them, but not in chronological order. In my view, kinship is a topic quite peripheral to Lévi-Strauss's main endeavour, and I shall consider it last.

There is, however, one general matter which cannot be ignored: for Lévi-Strauss, all his work is a defence and illustration of the structuralist method. Indeed, it is hard to say which of the two, Lévi-Strauss or structuralism, has made the other famous. But I shall argue in conclusion that in his case structuralism has become an uninspiring frame for an otherwise stimulating and inspired picture.

Untamed Thinking

At the very beginning of *The Savage Mind*, Lévi-Strauss argues against the notion that 'primitive' peoples are incapable of abstract thought. Many anthropologists would agree with him about this and cite as evidence the highly varied and elaborate moral and metaphysical concepts which have been recorded among such peoples throughout the world. Lévi-Strauss is fully aware of these concepts; he has himself analysed several, those of *mana* and *hau* for instance in his 'Introduction to the Work of Marcel Mauss'. Instead of these obvious cases, he chooses as evidence the Chinook language of the American Northwest, in which a proposition such as 'the bad man killed the poor child' is said to be rendered: 'the man's badness killed the child's poverty'. Thus, for Lévi-Strauss, the epitome of 'primitive' abstraction seems to be abstract synecdoche, his own favourite figure of speech! Perhaps this is not the best piece of evidence to choose, but it is certainly the most revealing of Lévi-Strauss's own turn of mind. However, this peculiar turn of mind is a source of incomparable insights into the underlying structure of folk classifications and folk narrative.

There is an interesting relationship between Lévi-Strauss's way of thinking and that of people who tell myths. It is one not of similarity but of complementarity: Lévi-Strauss tends, as we have seen, to represent a concrete object by one of its abstract properties; this makes him particularly apt at unravelling the thought of people who tend, contrarily, to represent an abstract property by some concrete object which possesses it, i.e. people given to using a 'concrete for abstract' form of synecdoche.

In traditional culture, abstractions such as moral qualities are often depicted concretely, in the guise of animal characters for instance; this is a well-known fact of which the peoples concerned are themselves often quite aware (the same mechanism is at work in contemporary culture too). If Lévi-Strauss's contribution had been merely to stress and illustrate this fact, he would be only one in a long line of scholars who, since antiquity, have been disputing whether fables are allegories based on metaphorical or synecdochal relationships, and what entities or notions they represent. At the end of the nineteenth century, for instance, followers of Max Müller argued that myths were allegories of the sun and of solar manifestations, against the followers of Adalbert Kuhn, who favoured thunder and storms.

Lévi-Strauss's approach is original in at least three ways. First, in its purpose: what he aims at understanding through the study of cultural symbolism is neither some primitive stage in human intellectual development nor the underlying ideology of a specific cultural area, but a mode of thinking shared by all humans, irrespective of time or place. Secondly, he is not concerned with ascribing a single interpretation to each symbol but rather with showing that symbols are open to a great variety of different and complementary interpretations. Thirdly, he is concerned with systematic relationships between symbols; the abstract level of interpretation is a means of establishing these relationships rather than an end in itself.

The translation of the French title *La Pensée sauvage* by *The Savage Mind* gives a false idea of Lévi-Strauss's general purpose. It suggests that there may be other kinds of human mind besides the 'savage' one, when in fact Lévi-Strauss has been one of the most systematic critics of this view in all its many guises. Since the book is about intellectual processes rather than their product, *pensée* should be translated as 'thinking' rather than 'mind' or 'thought'.

Sauvage has three standard translations: 'savage', 'wild', and 'untamed'. But Lévi-Strauss warns us that he does not mean *la pensée des sauvages* (the thinking of savages); for him *la pensée sauvage* is the way human beings—all human beings—think when they are not following explicit restrictive rules, or using aids and techniques such as writing or advanced calculus in order to increase both the quality and quantity of their intellectual output. In this respect 'untamed thinking' best conveys the sense of the French title, because it makes clear that there are not two types of mind but only one—which can be trained and put to particular uses (such as modern scientific investigation).

There is no disputing that much can be learned about human thinking in general by observing and experimenting with members of our own society. Nevertheless, it is reasonable to assume that some human intellectual abilities and dispositions might go unrecorded or be wrongly attributed if 'untamed' thinking and its products were ignored. Besides being interesting ethnographically, the study of societies which lack writing has a general psychological relevance: in them, intellectual mechanisms operate relatively unaided by artificial memory, and unguided by formal teaching. It is not that members of those societies are any closer to human nature: each and every one of us is as close to human nature as it is possible to be. It is that the product of natural abilities is less confused with that of artificial devices.

We may contrast Lévi-Strauss's approach here with the two basic views which each in turn have dominated anthropology. Not so long ago, exotic peoples were thought to be psychologically different from ourselves, so that to study them was of psychological relevance from both an evolutionary and a comparative point of view. More recently, the psychic unity of mankind has been generally recognized and used as an argument to separate anthropology from psychology: since the human mind is everywhere the same, anthropologists should not burden themselves with a study that can be carried out at home (where there are no mosquitoes). Lévi-Strauss's originality, which might easily go unnoticed or be misunderstood, is to have combined this notion of the psychic unity of man (actually, he has strengthened it) with new arguments to show that ethnography has a true, indeed unique, psychological relevance.

The 'proper' interpretation of symbols is a pursuit long practised in the West. In medieval hermeneutics, it had a strongly
normative character; in modern anthropology and comparative
religion, it purports to be strictly descriptive. But the mere idea
that there is or can be a 'proper' interpretation for symbols is itself
normative, when in most societies individuals are left fairly free to
interpret symbols as they please. If the scholar's purpose is to
throw light on what people do think rather than what they should
think, then the classical approach needs to be revised.

One of Lévi-Strauss's greatest claims to originality is to have
undertaken such a revision and developed an alternative to the
various rival methods of deciphering symbols. But, once again, the
way in which he describes his approach may be misleading. Faithful to the terminology of Saussure, he tends to refer to symbolic
phenomena as 'signifiers', and one might assume that the investigation is into an underlying code which pairs these signifiers with
their 'signifieds'. Yet, if the reader begins looking for the signifieds,
he soon realizes that the underlying code relates signifiers to other
signifiers: there *are* no signifieds. Everything is meaningful,
nothing is meant.

What Lévi-Strauss actually does is neither to decipher symbols
nor to describe a symbolic code. Rather, he attempts to show in
what ways natural and social phenomena lend themselves to intellectual elaboration, what selection of features this involves, and
what kind of mental associations can thus be established.

Any object in the world has an indefinite number of features.
Only some of these ever attract our attention and even fewer of
them when we attend to the object with some special aim in mind.
Thus different features of an animal, say, will be taken into consideration depending on whether we are concerned to know to which
taxonomic category it belongs, whether it is edible, whether it
is dangerous, whether it is worth photographing. It is often
claimed that the concerns of technologically primitive people are
overwhelmingly practical, and one would therefore expect them to
pay almost exclusive attention to such features in animals as
edibility or the danger they represent to man. But this is very far
from being the case. Modern scientific or technical thinking pays
attention to features selected according to strict criteria of relevance. But 'untamed' thinking seems to be indifferent to relevance,

or rather to have a much wider notion of it. Thus, contrary to expectation, most peoples in the world pay more attention to what animals eat than to which animals can be eaten.

Many pages of *The Savage Mind* are devoted to illustrating the endless variety of interest which humans everywhere take in their environment. The Navajo Indians, for example, are concerned with the way in which animals move; they classify them according to such features as whether they run, fly, or crawl; whether they travel by land or by water; whether they travel by day or by night. For the Ojibwa Indians a relevant feature of the squirrel is that it inhabits cedar trees; the Fang of the Gabon are concerned with the fact that squirrels take shelter in the holes of trees rather than with the species of the tree.

The Asmat of New Guinea have yet another viewpoint: 'Parrots and squirrels are famous fruit-eaters . . . and men about to go headhunting feel a relationship to these beings and call themselves their brothers . . . [because of the] parallelism between the human body and a tree, the human head and its fruits' (Zegwaard, quoted in *The Savage Mind*). For Westerners the comparison between the human head and fruit would as a matter of course be based on shape, and the analogy according to which heads are to bodies what fruit are to trees would seem superfluous and contrived. Not so for the Asmat: from a headhunter's point of view, heads are a detachable and valuable upper appendage of the body, a relationship analogous to that between fruit and tree, as seen by fruit-eaters. This interpretation is corroborated when we learn from Zegwaard's account that the victim's brain was ritually eaten and that it is said that 'the human head also has a hard shell which protects the core like a coconut'.

Since any object has an indefinite number of features, it can enter into an indefinite number of associations with an indefinite number of other objects. A given culture may highlight some of these features and associations, while the others remain merely potential. Although they are not spelled out, some of these extra associations may be strongly suggested by the structure of myth or ritual; others still may be brought into play by creative individuals who add to ritual rules or transform myths in the course of transmitting them. Given this, the anthropologist should not only record the explicit associations of standard symbols but also pay attention to the culturally salient features of a much wider range of phenomena.

In traditional 'keys' to symbols, whether popular or scholarly, items are considered one by one and each is given its proper interpretation either by fiat or according to some preconceived notion of what the symbol *must* mean. But when attempting an unprejudiced description, there is no way of deciding, for each item separately, which of its many features would be salient in a given culture. If, instead, relationships between items are considered, then shared or contrasted features stand out as the basis for symbolic associations. The greater the number of items related, the fewer the features which are likely to play a role: one should study not symbols but symbolic systems.

It is by thus looking for systems of relationships that Lévi-Strauss came to take a new interest in an old anthropological question, that of totemism. His short book, *Totemism*, and the chapters on this topic in *The Savage Mind* provide an excellent illustration of this aspect of his work.

By 'totemism' we usually mean a combination of features: a belief in a special relationship between an animal or plant (called the totem) on the one hand and a human group or individual on the other; prohibitions in the relationships of humans to their totem; specific rituals; and sometimes also a belief that the totem is the ancestor of the group, totemic group exogamy, etc. At the end of the nineteenth and at the beginning of the twentieth centuries, totemism was much discussed; it was believed by some anthropologists to be the source of religion, by most to be a stage in human evolution. However, almost from the start, a few authors questioned its homogeneity and saw it either as an ill-defined part of a wider phenomenon or as the illegitimate lumping together of independent features. Lévi-Strauss develops both criticisms: for him, 'totemism' denotes the contingent co-occurrence of sundry manifestations of a general human propensity to classify. Anthropologists have tended to lose interest in what they see as an inadequate notion, but by the same token they have ceased to pay sufficient attention to the forms of classification totemism was meant to encompass. Lévi-Strauss's aim is to reconsider these classifications from a different point of view.

If the question asked were: 'why should a given social group consider itself to stand in a special relationship to, say, eagles?", only unsatisfactory answers could be given: 'because they are mistaken about their ancestry', or 'because they think they resemble eagles and assume this implies a relationship'. Explaining strange behaviour by even stranger intellectual errors is no explanation at all.

The question could be reframed: 'why should a society consider that each of its constituent groups stands in a special relationship to a different species of animals?' Now it is the whole set—and not just one—of the dyadic (i.e. twofold) relationships between social groups and animal species that is taken into account. This opens up a choice of perspectives: the over-all picture can be redrawn as a single dyadic relationship between the two sets: of social groups and animal species. Animals can now be considered as emblems of proper names used to individuate human groups. The social set is mapped on to the animal set to this end. This is the beginning of an explanation but it is not yet sufficient. If this were all, why not use arbitrary names? Why use animals? Why so much content when pure form would do just as well?

Lévi-Strauss points out that the human–animal relationship can be understood in a third, even more systematic way: neither as a set of dyadic relationships between individual items, nor as a dyadic relationship between sets of individual items, but as a second-degree dyadic relationship between two sets of first-degree relationships:

> On the one hand there are animals which differ from each other (in that they belong to distinct species, each of which has its own physical appearance and mode of life), and on the other hand there are men . . . who also differ from each other (in that they are distributed among different segments of the society, each occupying a particular position in the social structure). The resemblance presupposed by so-called totemic representations is *between these two systems of differences*.

(*Totemism*)

Seen in this light, the recourse to animal species provides a unique system of differences: they do not overlap, they look different, they live differently, they offer an endless choice of opposed features that can be used to contrast human groups.

'Totemic' beliefs and rituals may highlight some of these features. For instance:

> The following clans stand in a joking relationship to each other among the Luapula [of Zambia]: the Leopard and the Goat clans, because the leopards eat goats, the Mushroom and the Anthill clans because mushrooms grow on anthills, the Mush and Goat clans because men like meat in their mush, the Elephant and Clay clans because women in the old days used to carve out elephants' footprints from the ground and use these natural shapes as receptacles instead of fashioning pots.
>
> (*The Savage Mind*)

Here the joking relationship between clans is based on specific features of the relationship between totems. Formal proper names could not be exploited in this way. Indeed, in such a case, form and content cannot be dissociated.

Even without such explicit elaborations, the system may suggest giving special importance to certain implicit features. If, for instance, a tribe were divided into three clans named after the eagle, the bear, and the turtle, this might suggest that we concentrate on the natural element of each of these species, and further contrast the three clans as associated with sky, earth, and water.

It might seem that the system of differences between animal species is too powerful to match the much weaker differences between human groups. Members of the same society look alike and live in similar ways and conditions; social groups do not differ in the ways natural species do. But the point precisely is that human groups are trying through 'totemic' institutions not to match two pre-existing systems of differences, but rather to build one system with the help of the other. They are trying not so much to *express* social differences as to create or strengthen them. In this respect the force of the animal system is never excessive; whatever aspects of it can be mapped on to the social system are welcome.

Thus understood, the symbolic potential of 'totemic' animals appears both systematic and quite open-ended. There can be no question of ascribing a proper interpretation to each animal: on the one hand they cannot be interpreted outside their mutual relationship; on the other hand no relationship can exhaust their potential as a source of relationships, nor any one interpretation exhaust their interpretative potential.

This superior, Lévi-Straussian account of totemism depends, however, on certain psychological assumptions. Earlier accounts assumed that human beings make intellectual mistakes or that they have a use for naming systems. Neither assumption is extravagant. Lévi-Strauss further assumes that the human mind is able and liable to impose a specific kind of organization on its representation of the world. This is a clear step away from the strict empiricist view of learning prevalent in modern anthropology and many scholars have objected to it. Myself, I would argue that we may need to go even further in this new, rationalist direction.

I would also argue that Lévi-Strauss's approach to totemism and more generally to symbolism has renewed the issues in a most important and positive way. Lévi-Strauss assumes that the structure of such symbolic systems as totemic classification is determined by a universal human ability rather than by the inabilities of 'primitives', or by practical need, whether individual or social. He neatly summarizes this when he says that symbolic animals are chosen not because they are 'good to eat', but because they are 'good to think'—one could paraphrase this: not because they are food but because they are food for thought.

Suppose one knew little about a particular organism's digestive system but had the good fortune to discover that a specific range of foodstuffs was optimal for it; one could then make new and interesting assumptions about that digestive system. Now, if Lévi-Strauss is right and cultural symbols such as totems are optimal food for thought, then their study offers us a new approach to the study of the human mind; conversely, the study of the human mind can throw new light on cultural symbolism. The use Lévi-Strauss makes of these new perspectives is sometimes seminal, sometimes unconvincing; but this matters less than the fact of his having opened them up.

Myth

The four volumes of *Mythologiques* are a monumental illustration and development of the central idea in *The Savage Mind*: that concrete categories can serve as intellectual tools to express abstract notions and relationships; and that 'untamed' thinking tends to order its world in this way.

Most cultural phenomena, such as technology or political

organization, must submit to a variety of ecological and sociological constraints. By contrast, myths—orally transmitted and culturally selected narratives—tend to ignore any determinations other than intellectual ones, and even these seem to remain relatively loose. Hence myths should provide an exceptional insight into the spontaneous working of the human mind. To expand on this premise, Lévi-Strauss reviews in *Mythologiques* more than 800 American Indian myths and a wealth of other ethnographical data. Each myth is considered in relation to many others. The resulting web is too intricate to try and cut off one fragment from it. Rather, in order to illustrate Lévi-Strauss's approach and to develop certain criticisms of it, I shall start from a much shorter and more modest text, a paper entitled 'Four Winnebago Myths: A Structural Sketch' (originally published in *Culture and History: Essays in honor of Paul Radin*, ed. J. Diamond, 1960).

Under the title *The Culture of the Winnebago: as Described by Themselves* (1949), the American anthropologist Paul Radin published four myths which he had collected among this Indian people. Lévi-Strauss's aim is to show that these myths were even more closely related to each other than Radin himself had realized. The argument concerns more particularly the fourth myth which, to Radin, appeared quite atypical; indeed at first sight, it seems not to belong with the other three at all. Here is my own summary of this fourth myth (material in inverted commas is quoted from Radin):

An orphan boy, a good hunter like his father, lived with his grandmother at the end of a village. The daughter of the village chief saw him and fell in love with him: 'would that he would take liberties with me or that he would say a word to me or court me. This is what she earnestly desired, indeed this she constantly thought of. The boy was still somewhat immature and never said a word to her'. She did not dare speak and after a long time spent in unhappy yearning, she fell ill and died. On top of her grave dirt was piled so that nothing could seep through.

Out of grief, the chief decided to move with all the villagers to a place several days' journey away. The orphan boy, however, did not want to go for fear that the hunting would not be as good there. With the permission of the chief, he and his grandmother stayed behind to take care of the chief's daughter's grave. Before leaving, the chief had the floor of their lodge covered with dirt to keep it warm.

The orphan, who could 'not yet pack animals very far', hunted in the vicinity, avoiding the old village. One evening, having chased his wounded quarry further than usual and returning late, he crossed the village and noticed a light in the old chief's house. Inside he saw the chief's daughter's ghost, who told him why she had died, and added: 'because of thus behaving, I am dead, but my ghost has not yet departed to the place where the ghosts go. I beseech you, try to help me this time'. To bring her back to life, she told him, he would have to submit to a test: he must spend four nights in the chief's house. Each night he must try to fight off sleep by telling stories in front of a big fire. When he felt too sleepy and lay down, 'you will have the sensation as though something was crawling over your body; but they will not be insects doing it. Do not under any conditions grab for the place itching'. Although each night it was more difficult, the orphan boy succeeded in passing the test. The ghosts who had been torturing him let him go, and he was able to restore the girl to life, to bring her to his house and to marry her.

Having heard the news, the villagers returned. The young wife soon gave birth to a boy. 'Now when the boy was able to shoot real arrows, then the husband spoke to his wife and said, "Although I am not yet old, I have been here on earth as long as I can. . . . However, I shall not die as you did; I shall simply go home, just so."' She chose to go with him, and they both became wolves and lived under the earth. Sometimes they come back to this earth to bless an Indian when he fasts.

As is often the case with myths, the episodes here seem to follow each other without really following *from* each other; the causal links are weak. Many details (many more in the full text) seem unnecessary. Until recently, mythologists tended to think that myths were indeed loosely organized and consisted largely in ornamental flourishes. Against this Lévi-Strauss argues that there is more structure to a myth than the mere narrative succession of episodes. There is a whole system of correspondences among the elements of the myth, over and above their chronological order.

Thus in this particular myth, the orphan boy and the chief's daughter are at opposite ends of the social scale, but from a natural point of view, argues Lévi-Strauss, their positions are reversed: the girl is 'paralysed when it comes to expressing her feelings'; she is 'a defective human being, lacking an essential attribute of life'. As for the boy, 'he is a miraculous hunter, i.e. he entertains privileged relations with the natural world, the world of animals.'

Therefore may we claim that the myth actually confronts us with a polar system consisting in two individuals, one male, the other female, and both exceptional in so far as each of them is overgifted in one way and under-gifted in the other. . . . The plot consists in carrying this disequilibrium to its logical extreme; the girl dies a *natural* death, the boy stays alone, i.e. he also dies but in a *social* way. . . . Their positions are inverted: the girl is below (in her grave), the boy above (in his lodge).

This last opposition is confirmed by the apparently superfluous detail of dirt being piled on the grave in one case, and on the floor of the lodge in the other, which 'emphasizes that, relative to the earth's surface, i.e. dirt, the boy is now above and the girl below'. 'This new equilibrium, however, will be no more lasting than the first. *She who was unable to live cannot die*; her ghost lingers "on earth". . . . With a wonderful symmetry, the boy will meet, a few years later, with a similar although inverted fate. . . . *He who overcame death proves unable to live*' (Lévi-Strauss's italics).

Lévi-Strauss's own analysis is not the only Lévi-Straussian analysis that could be made of the myth. Some of his assumptions I find unconvincing: the girl's shyness at speaking her feelings need not be seen as a *natural* disability; nor does anything in the text seem to justify Lévi-Strauss's contention that the youth is a 'miraculous' hunter: he does not perform unusual hunting feats; he cannot even 'pack animals very far', and he is never praised as an exceptional hunter. Hence the opposition between the girl and the youth in terms of their natural gifts seems overstated. Again, calling the fact that the orphan boy remains alone with his grandmother a 'social death' may be to impose a Western metaphor on Winnebago thinking.

There are other parallelisms and oppositions in the myth which Lévi-Strauss has not chosen to dwell upon. But this type of analysis should be understood as an investigation of the *potential* which a myth offers rather than the ascription to it of a single definitive pattern. The claim underlying Lévi-Strauss's approach is that complex outputs of 'untamed' thinking, e.g. myths, exhibit this kind of potential to a unique degree.

To some extent we can each make a different use of this potential, and it may be that the anthropologist's use of it never quite matches that of any native. However, the mythologist's aim is to give an account of the potential itself, not of its actual uses; and, adds Lévi-Strauss (somewhat overstating the case), 'if the final aim of anthropology is to contribute to a better knowledge of objectified thought and its mechanisms, it is in the last resort immaterial whether ... the thought processes of ... American Indians take shape through the medium of my thought or whether mine take place through the medium of theirs' (*The Raw and the Cooked*).

Showing that myths have a more complex internal structure than meets the ear is only the first part of Lévi-Strauss's programme. The second part has to do with what may be called the 'external structure' of a myth. Mythologists long ago established that there are strong resemblances to be found between different myths, and argument has raged as to whether these resemblances reflect common origins, identical stages in cultural evolution, or universal categories of the human mind. Lévi-Strauss's contribution has been, first, to show that resemblances are not the only close links to be found between myths. Similarity is one type of systematic relationship between them; inversion is another. Some myths are related to others in differing from them in a systematic way.

Further, Lévi-Strauss argues that myths should not be analysed one by one, but only as part of a group of related myths. Thus some aspects of the myth we have just analysed come out only when another Winnebago myth, the first in Radin's collection, is also taken into account. Here is my summary of this myth:

A chief's son spent his time fasting in order 'to acquire some powers from those various beings called the sacred ones. ... After a while he established a bond-friendship ... devotedly he loved his friend'. One day the chief's son was told that a war party was about to set out but was forbidden to tell anybody. He nevertheless told his friend and they both joined the warriors. The two friends fought with great bravery and were feasted by the villagers when they returned. They both became great warriors, married and went to live in their own lodges away from the village. Whenever they came into the village 'Meticulous was the care bestowed upon them. Because of their accomplishments in war, the village had been greatly benefited by these two and they were honoured and respected'.

One day, as they were about to set out on an expedition far afield for the sake of the villagers, they were ambushed and killed after much fighting. Their ghosts returned to the village only to realize to their dismay that they had become invisible. They attended the Four Nights Wake celebrated for them, before setting out on their journey to the land of ghosts. The chief's son's friend was so moved by the villagers' grief that he insisted they find a way to return. The chief's son said it could be done if they passed a test while on their journey. They travelled and arrived in the first ghost village. There they were extremely well received by beautiful men and women and a dance was held which lasted all night. However, the chief's son warned his friend: 'never get up to dance with them. If you get up you will not attain your goal'. This was repeated for four nights and each night proved more difficult. Then the four nights of dancing were repeated in three other villages and each time it was more difficult to resist the urge to join the dancers; but in the end they succeeded and could travel to the house of the Earthmaker. The Earthmaker gave them a choice of where to live. They chose their original village and were reborn, each in his own family. 'And then, in the course of time they met each other and recognized each other although they were infants and although they were being carried by others . . . they enjoyed this recognition very much. . . . As they grew older they repeated what they had done in their previous existence.'

What does this myth have to do with the earlier one? In both there is a death and a resurrection, but there the parallel seems to end. The characters, circumstances, and mood of the two myths are otherwise quite different. On closer inspection, however, these seemingly random differences turn out to be systematic symmetries and oppositions. I shall give my own account of these, borrowing freely from Lévi-Strauss.

The moods are not just different, they are opposed: in the first myth the heroes submit to their sad fate; in the second, they improve on their already glorious destiny. In the first they are inordinately slow, the girl to speak, the boy to mature, and they lack mobility; in the second they become warriors (i.e. 'real men' in Winnebago terms) while still too young to be included normally in a war party; their moral and physical development is inordinately rapid and they are also extremely mobile, choosing to live away from the village, and to go on distant expeditions. Both myths have a cyclical character, but in the first case the cycle goes from one generation to the next (the orphan boy eventually leaves behind him another orphan boy); whereas in the second it is the same happy pair of heroes who start their lives all over again. Generally speaking, the mood of the first myth is slow, sad, and subdued, that of the second fast, joyful, and triumphant.

The relationships of symmetry and inversion between the two myths can be expressed in tabular form:

a chief's daughter falls in love	a chief's son makes a friend
she keeps silent when she should speak	he speaks when he should have kept silent
as a result of which she suffers and dies	as a result of which they fight and kill
the villagers leave the hero behind and go to live at a distance	the heroes leave the villagers behind and go to live at a distance
on one occasion the hero has to go further afield than usual to kill his quarry	on one occasion the two heroes are about to go further afield than usual and get killed
the hero comes back through the village and sees the ghost of the heroine	the heroes come back to the village and cannot be seen
to bring the heroine back to life the hero must undergo a four-night trial in the same spot	to bring themselves back to life the heroes must undergo a four-night trial four times in four different places
the trial consists in resisting the temptation to get rid of aggressive ghosts who have a repulsive non-human appearance and behaviour	the trial consists in resisting the temptation to join friendly ghosts who have an attractive, quite human appearance and behaviour
the hero succeeds, the heroine is resurrected, the villagers return	the heroes succeed and return to their village
the heroes give birth to a child	the heroes are born again as children
in spite of this resurrection the heroes cannot live, and become wolf-spirits, the protectors of fasters	thanks to this resurrection the heroes can live their lives again (for the chief's son this is marked by much fasting)

Both myths display extraordinary characters and events. Their heroes neither live nor die in the way ordinary people do. They achieve a kind of immortality, but in two quite different ways: the orphan boy and the chief's daughter by neither quite living nor quite dying; the warrior heroes by living and dying over and over again. These symmetrically opposed extraordinary fates provide points of comparison for a Winnebago view of human life and death.

Such an understanding can be reached only if we examine groups of myths, not isolated myths. Many features of a particular myth stand out only in relation to other myths. Their potential as a source of patterns is increased and becomes specific when we compare them. The anthropologist's task is to throw light on this potential, not to describe what use is or should be made of it. The analysis I have given above is not the only one that could be devised for the myth in question; if other myths were taken into account, other patterns of relationships would become apparent. Assuming that the same is true of all culturally related myths, the question then is: What follows from it? What can we learn from this potential in myths and groups of myths to yield such patterns?

Lévi-Strauss likes to claim that he has shown 'wonderful symmetries', 'perfect homologies' or 'complete inversions' in myths, but it would be fairer to say that if his descriptions of them are often truly 'wonderful', the relations he describes are not. 'Perfect symmetries' are achieved only by ignoring some of the data and by re-describing the rest in terms of carefully selected abstract synecdoches. But if we leave aside these exaggerations, there remains the exciting suspicion that the fleeting shapes and contours one can glimpse through the mist are those of a true *terra incognita*. It is not to belittle Lévi-Strauss's theoretical contribution to suggest that he may be first and foremost a discoverer of facts—the explorer of a mental continent which he is not to be reproached for having failed so far to chart fully.

Lévi-Strauss often talks as if he had discovered a new language. Sometimes, however, he offers more promising suggestions. Many metaphorical observations about mythology can be stated in linguistic terms. If these are taken literally, though, many of them become either meaningless or hopelessly paradoxical. If the related myths studied in *Mythologiques* are part of a single language, then each American Indian society has access to only a very small sample of messages in that language; nobody (except possibly Lévi-Strauss himself) could be said to be even remotely fluent in it; and what kind of a language is that?

As a structuralist, Lévi-Strauss should expect the analysis of a language to consist in identifying its minimal elements and then determining how these combine. He has indeed coined a term, 'mytheme', for the minimal units of a myth, but thereafter has failed to employ it. He has never put forward anything at all resembling a grammar of myths. Some of his pupils have tried to develop 'linguistic' models, but he has paid no obvious attention to researches he himself had inspired.

If myths were a language, then the question of meaning would arise. Lévi-Strauss's approach to this question is first to organize the systems of correspondences underlying myths into separate 'codes': for instance, in the myths analysed above, the heroes' travels and their changing locations could be said to pertain to a spatial code, and the social links involved—parenthood, marriage, chiefship, friendship, etc.—to a social one. The relationships between elements within each code are then shown to correspond to those in other codes, and a complex pattern of such correspondences can be drawn up, displaying various levels of relationship: between elements, between codes, between episodes from the same myth, between myths, and so on. Lévi-Strauss calls these 'meaning' relationships (notwithstanding the fact that they are reciprocal, whereas the relation of a signifier and a signified is not), and the system of such relationships a 'matrix' of meanings:

Each matrix of meanings refers to another matrix, each myth to other myths. And if it is now asked to what final meaning these mutually significative meanings are referring—since in the last resort and in their totality they must refer to something—the only reply to emerge from this study is that myths signify the mind that evolves them by making use of the world of which it is itself a part.

(The Raw and the Cooked)

This cryptic statement may be clarified a little by another remark: 'When the mind is left to commune with itself [as in myth, which "has no obvious practical function"] and no longer has to come to terms with objects, it is in a sense reduced to imitating itself as object' (ibid.). One could say, similarly, that in gymnastics the human body fulfils no obvious external function and is in a sense reduced to imitating itself. But this is a display rather than a coding. Similarly, assuming that fundamental mental mechanisms are displayed in myths, it does not follow that they are thereby *signified*.

It is because Lévi-Strauss assumes *a priori* that meaning relationships must be at the core of mythical thought that he inserts them forcibly, although there is nothing in his empirical findings to justify his doing so. On the contrary, it can be claimed[1] that one of Lévi-Strauss's greatest achievements in his treatment of myth (and of symbolism in general) is to have made it possible to dispense with the notion of meaning. If I am right, then this is one achievement which Lévi-Strauss not only does not claim but implicitly *dis*claims, and this makes it particularly difficult to understand or assess his contribution to the study of myth.

Scattered through his books and articles are a variety of suggested alternatives to the linguistic model. A myth, he maintains repeatedly, is the transformation of other myths. This is meant in two senses: it is a genetic transformation, in that a myth-teller never creates his narrative *ex nihilo* but tells stories he has heard before, whether or not he is aware of the modifications he is almost bound to introduce into them; and it is an intellectual transformation, in that, as we have seen, a myth is related to other myths and can be 'transformed' into any of these by a number of more or less regular modifications, such as symmetrical inversion.

Now, we have very little and incomplete empirical data about the actual genetic transformations which myths undergo. One would need to follow myth-tellers throughout their lives, to be present when they hear a myth, present again when they retell it; and then do the same with the succeeding generation of myth-tellers. What Lévi-Strauss's work suggests is that although we cannot observe actual transformations in this way, we can try and reconstruct them experimentally: we can take intellectual transformations between related myths as hypothetical models for genetic transformations. This assumes that the modifications which the myth-teller is likely to make are not random departures from what he has heard but tend rather to consist in homologous replacements, symmetrical inversions, and so on. If this is the case, the regularities in the resulting myths could be accounted for by the actual process of their formation and transformation; it is as if oral transmission (with the demands it makes on memory and attention) selected over a period of time regular forms in individual myths and regular relationships among myths belonging to the

[1] See my *Rethinking Symbolism* (1975), ch.3.

same culture. Viewed in this light, the facts brought out by Lévi-Strauss—all those odd correspondences and regularities—could possibly be accounted for as ideal properties for 'untamed' thinking (more specifically, I would add, for storage and retrieval). The study of myth could then throw light on little-known aspects of the human mind.

Kinship

Lévi-Strauss achieved professional recognition by his work on kinship; and general recognition by his defence of structuralism. Yet it can be argued, without disparagement, that as his contribution to anthropology has developed these two aspects have lost much of their central importance.

The Elementary Structures of Kinship of 1949 was to have been followed by a further volume on complex structures, but we are still waiting for that. It might have clarified the scope of Lévi-Strauss's theory of kinship and its significance for his view of the human mind. In its present, impressive yet incomplete, state, his work on kinship stands somewhat apart. On the other hand, Lévi-Strauss seems to have exhausted all that he had to say on the subject of structuralism. There is no reason to doubt that structuralist methodology played a major role in the elaboration of his views, but this is of historical rather than theoretical importance. From a theoretical point of view, Lévi-Strauss's structuralism is, I shall maintain, an odd mixture of sound principles and unsound expectations. It may have served a purpose, but by now it has become a hindrance to the full development of his own anthropological insights.

Writing of Lévi-Strauss's theory of kinship, Edmund Leach warns us: 'This is technical anthropological stuff and readers who prefer a diet of soufflé to suet pudding must mind their digestion' (*Lévi-Strauss*, 1970). And indeed, the technicalities of the topic are such that a hundred pages would not be enough to give a meaningful summary of it to lay readers. Here, therefore, I cannot do more than point to a few links between Lévi-Strauss's work on kinship and his more general interests.

In all human societies there exist rules about whom one can and whom one cannot marry. Some of these rules concern categories of relations, e.g., men may be forbidden to marry their *sisters* but allowed to marry their *cousins* ('sisters' and 'cousins' are italicized here since they stand for English native categories, not anthropological terms). Rather than merely forbidding or allowing, such rules may also take a more positive form: positive marriage rules state (more or less compellingly) that spouses should be chosen from among a given category, e.g., 'a man should marry one of his *nam*' (a Kachin native category for 'matrilateral cross-cousins', in anthropological jargon).

For Lévi-Strauss, the condition which makes a kinship structure 'elementary' is that it should include a positive marriage rule of this kind. His approach to elementary structures of kinship was original in four main respects:
(a) He undertook to synthesize the available data on an unprecedented scale, and put forward a systematic classification of it. In his own words:

Behind what seemed to be the superficial contingency and incoherent diversity of the laws governing marriage, I discerned a small number of simple principles, thanks to which a very complex mass of customs and practices, at first sight absurd (and generally held to be so), could be reduced to a meaningful system.

(The Raw and the Cooked)

This is an exaggeration in two respects: firstly, it is the elementary structures and not the laws governing marriage that are 'reduced to a meaningful system'; secondly, other anthropologists had already brought some order to the chaos. But despite these qualifications, Lévi-Strauss has advanced the systematic ordering of the data much further than any of his predecessors.
(b) Lévi-Strauss has developed the idea that, in elementary structures, the positive marriage rule is at the core of many institutions: relationships between descent groups, symbolic ordering of the society, cultural attitudes, etc. This is most clearly the case when the native categories used to refer to relatives themselves suggest the positive marriage rule. For instance, if the term *tsa*, used for a man's mother's brother, also means his wife's father, this suggests that a proper marriage is one that takes place with the mother's brother's daughter. When all in-laws are consistently called by terms used for kin—that is to say when there is no terminological distinction between kin and in-laws—both the way in which rela-

tionships work and the way in which people conceive of them are bound to be affected. One of the most novel and valuable aspects of Lévi-Strauss's work has been to pay systematic attention to the close connection between positive marriage rules and these peculiar terminologies, and to show how, together, they are central to a whole set of institutions and cultural representations.

(c) A third source of originality in Lévi-Strauss's approach was his attempt to account for kinship structures in terms of basic mental structures:

What are the mental structures to which we have referred and the universality of which can be established? It seems there are three: the exigency of the rule as a rule; the notion of reciprocity regarded as the most immediate form of integrating the opposition between the self and others; and finally the synthetic nature of the gift, i.e., that the agreed transfer of a valuable from one individual to another makes these individuals into partners, and adds a new quality to the valuable transferred.

(The Elementary Structures of Kinship)

Lévi-Strauss's systematic classification of positive marriage rules is based on 'the principle of reciprocity'. His integration of various aspects of kinship around the marriage rule is largely related to 'the synthetic nature of the gift'. But it could not be claimed that he has done more in this connection than show a certain congruence between very general principles and specific social forms. The psychological import of his conclusions is unclear and, conversely, psychological considerations could hardly modify his conclusions. Lévi-Strauss has himself explained why this should be so. In *Elementary Structures*, he says, 'there was nothing to guarantee that the [kinship] obligations came from within. Perhaps they were merely the reflections in men's minds of certain social demands that had been objectified in institutions' *(The Raw and the Cooked)*. He then goes on to argue, quite soundly, that the study of myths should be much more directly relevant to the understanding of the human mind.

(d) A fourth source of originality in Lévi-Strauss's approach is implied in the actual title of his book, *The Elementary Structures of Kinship*: he holds that marriage systems based on a positive rule are *elementary*; their study should serve as the basis for a general theory of kinship. These systems are elementary in that the principles on which they openly organize the 'circulation of women' are at work in all societies. In complex structures these principles are lost to view among many other factors.

Strong doubts have been expressed about the possibility of generalizing from elementary structures to kinship in general, most notably by the British anthropologists Rodney Needham and Edmund Leach. Until such time as a study of complex structures has satisfactorily established that 'elementary' structures are truly elementary, the onus of proof is on Lévi-Strauss. Scepticism on this matter need not be taken as a belittlement of his work. A study which throws light on the several hundred known 'elementary' systems is no mean feat in itself; furthermore, its general anthropological relevance need neither be centred on, nor limited to, kinship. For instance Lévi-Strauss's elaboration of the principle of 'reciprocity' has inspired further research on economico-ritual systems.

It seems clear that the issue remains open: more generally, a lot remains to be settled about the links between Lévi-Strauss's work on kinship and what has become, both in bulk and importance, the central aspect of his contribution to thought: his anthropological approach to the study of the human mind.

Structuralism

The word 'structuralism' has suffered from its popularity; it has been used in many different senses and sometimes with no sense at all. My favourite example of its misuse occurred in the heat of the 'May events' in France in 1968, when a leading French football coach declared that those responsible needed to 'revise the structuralism' of the national team. Given this variety of application, I shall limit myself to some of Lévi-Strauss's own uses of the term and not inquire whether—or how—they connect up with its other uses. There is however one connection which Lévi-Strauss himself stresses: that with structuralist, Saussurian, linguistics.

Three principles of this tradition have been particularly relevant to the development of Lévi-Strauss's views. Firstly, language is to be studied in itself before we turn to studying its relationship to other systems (historical, sociological, or psychological): internal structure takes precedence over external functions. Secondly, speech, the audible manifestation of language, is to be broken down into a finite number of minimal elements, such as phonemes on the phonological level. Thirdly, the elements of a language are to be defined by their mutual relationships. These relationships are of two kinds: paradigmatic relationships between elements which can be substituted for each other; syntagmatic relationships between elements which can combine together. Lévi-Strauss has adapted these three principles to his own anthropological ends.

When generalized, the first principle states that a proper object for scientific investigation must be a set of data having internal coherence and external autonomy. Selecting such a set is a crucial first step. Lévi-Strauss's criticism of earlier views on totemism is precisely this: that the set of facts which had been brought together did not have the required coherence and autonomy. Of this first principle, Lévi-Strauss can quite rightly claim that it is a part of scientific method in general. By stressing it, he has helped to introduce a greater concern for methodological soundness among anthropologists. At the same time, since the principle can hardly be controverted (anthropologists of the past were guilty only of neglect), it does not distinguish structuralist methodology from scientific methodology in general. If, as Lévi-Strauss sometimes seems to be claiming, structuralism means nothing more than a scientific approach, we should rapidly drop the term and go back to 'scientific', to avoid football coaches and others becoming utterly confused.

The search for minimal elements, although Lévi-Strauss claims it is an essential step in anthropology also, plays only a minor role in his actual research. I have already noted that he coined a term 'mytheme' for the minimal units of a myth, and then failed to make use of it. He has also asserted the existence of 'atoms of kinship', and built interesting hypotheses around them, but this atom is neither minimal nor an element in the way in which phonemes or morphemes are elements to a linguist. More generally, not everything in the world can be analysed into a finite set of 'minimal elements'; there are continuous functions, non-enumerable sets, and sets which can only be defined by general properties, without identification of their elements. There are also many cases—and, judging from Lévi-Strauss's actual practice, myth is one of them—where to look for minimal elements is not the best approach. The structuralist expectation that any coherent and autonomous domain can be usefully divided up into a finite number of minimal elements is unwarranted.

The third principle is that a proper structural description should be a characterization of paradigmatic and syntagmatic relationships. When elements can be isolated, it is generally quite easy to order them in such a way. But in most cases (language being one of them if we accept Chomsky's critique of structuralism) such an ordering is of no great use—and why should it be? Here again is a principle which, apart from giving a few illustrations of it, Lévi-Strauss has been little concerned to follow.

To those three principles carried over from linguistics into anthropology, Lévi-Strauss has added a fourth: he claims that related structures should be formal transformations of each other, and that the rules governing these transformations constitute a more abstract and general level of analysis. The notion of 'transformation' can be understood in a very trivial sense, in that anything can be said to stand in a relationship of transformation with anything else; but this weak notion is of no relevance here. If we take a more specific notion of transformation, then we need compelling reasons to expect Lévi-Strauss's claim to stand up. In fact, two cases, those of mythical transformations and of mathematical models of kinship, could be said to illustrate that claim. In each of these cases, however, 'transformation' is specified quite differently.

It might well be asked why Lévi-Strauss should have bothered to put forward a 'structuralist' method based on principles which he himself does not feel impelled to follow. I can see two reasons for this. In the 1940s and '50s, many forward-looking scholars set great store by the development of a unified science of communication based on semiotics, cybernetics, and information theory. This science would bring together the study of language, culture, and society with that of the human brain and mind. Common concepts, and a common method, would lead to a new scientific take-off. Lévi-Strauss's early methodological papers were meant as contributions to this new science and he probably expected that they would soon be superseded by further advances along the same lines, made either by himself or by others.

Twenty years later, it has become quite clear that such expectations were largely unjustified. The important advances that have taken place in these particular fields owe little or nothing, except a jargon, to any unified science of communication. Because Lévi-Strauss has devoted himself to the furtherance of his own discipline, he has, in practice, left his earlier methodological optimism on one side. But hopes are not easily given up; he may believe that his expectations will still prove to have been justified and that there is no compelling reason why he should reconsider principles he has never yet properly exploited.

Secondly, Lévi-Strauss's structuralist stance must be understood in the context of the rationalist/empiricist controversy. In asserting that cultures have developed not simply in response to external demands but, more fundamentally, in accordance with the human mind's internal constraints, Lévi-Strauss took a major step away from empiricism. He did this at a time when empiricism exercised an almost total domination over the social and psychological sciences, under such labels as 'behaviourism' in psychology and 'cultural relativism' in anthropology. As a result he came under constant attack. Understandably, he chose to defend his first having taken this step rather than advancing further in the rationalist direction in which it was leading him. The very simple and homogeneous structures which structuralism postulates served to make this re-introduction of the human mind into anthropology much more acceptable. The 'structuralist' mind is as tidy as a crystal; it has no room for odd-looking or specialized 'innate devices'.

Writing in the late 1970s, it is clear that once one considers that the human mind is a proper subject of study—and why shouldn't it be?—there is no sense in laying down what kind or degree of structure one ought to find in it. It is hard to comprehend now why it was once thought that the brain must have a simpler structure than, say, the hand. The only way to follow up Lévi-Strauss's initial step towards a better understanding of the workings of the human mind is to eliminate any *a priori* limitations on what one is permitted to find. In this respect structuralism allows, paradoxically, for too little by way of structure.

There is one other important way in which Lévi-Strauss uses the word 'structuralism', and that is to refer to any general aspect of his own work. For instance, he would say that it was 'structuralist' to pay attention in myths as much to their systematic differences as to resemblances, or to refuse to be satisfied with a description of 'totemism' which accounts only for its form and not its content. Such an approach derives less from any original principles than from an intellectual attitude both bold and demanding. Together with his many profound insights, it is this attitude which has enabled Lévi-Strauss to make a truly general and also very personal contribution to anthropology in its widest sense. That he should attribute his own individual creativeness to an abstract 'structuralism' is modesty on his part. To follow him in this would be to show either submissiveness or ingratitude.

Bibliography

Claude Lévi-Strauss was born in 1908, and educated in Paris. From 1935 to 1939 he taught at the University of São Paulo in Brazil, and did anthropological field work in that country. Since 1959 he has been Professor of Social Anthropology at the Collège de France.

BOOKS

La Vie familiale et sociale des Indiens Nambikwara (Paris, 1948)

Les Structures élémentaires de la parenté (Paris, 1949); English translation, *The Elementary Structures of Kinship* (London and New York, 1969)

Race et histoire (Paris, 1952)

Tristes tropiques (Paris, 1955); English translation, *Tristes Tropiques* (London, 1973; New York, 1974)

Anthropologie structurale (Paris, 1958); English translation, *Structural Anthropology*, vol. I (New York, 1963; London, 1968); vol. II (New York, 1976; London, 1977)

Le Totémisme aujourd'hui (Paris, 1962); English translation, *Totemism* (Boston, 1963; London, 1964)

La Pensée sauvage (Paris, 1962); English translation, *The Savage Mind* (London and Chicago, 1966)

Le Cru et le cuit (Mythologiques I) (Paris, 1964); English translation, *The Raw and the Cooked* (London and New York, 1970)

Du miel aux cendres (Mythologiques II) (Paris, 1967); English translation, *From Honey to Ashes* (London and New York, 1973)

L'Origine des manières de table (Mythologiques III) (Paris, 1968); English translation, *The Origin of Table Manners* (London and New York, 1978)

L'Homme nu (Mythologiques IV) (Paris, 1971)
Anthropologie structurale deux (Paris, 1973)
La Voie des masques (Geneva, 1975)

There is a fine essay in English on Lévi-Strauss in the Modern Masters series: E. R. Leach, *Lévi-Strauss* (London, 1970; rev. edn., New York, 1974).

Georges Charbonnier's *Conversations avec Claude Lévi-Strauss* (Paris, 1961), in which Lévi-Strauss discusses his own work, has also been translated: *Conversations with Claude Lévi-Strauss* (London and New York, 1969).

Roland Barthes

JOHN STURROCK

Roland Barthes is an incomparable enlivener of the literary mind. He is as adventurous in the formulation of new principles for the understanding of literature as he is provocative in dispatching the old ones. To read him is to be led to think more intelligently and enjoyably about what literature is; about both the practice of writing and its function. He has renewed literary criticism in France, which is now a far more varied and practical discipline than it was, and is helping to renew it outside France as the translations of his work spread.

Barthes has not done this by constructing some definite theoretical position of his own *vis-à-vis* literature and then sticking to it stubbornly over the years. Quite the reverse; he is famous for his mobility, for the way in which he is constantly transcending old positions, and often in unexpected directions. Each new book that he publishes is very obviously a departure, not a consolidation of his earlier arguments. There *is* a consistency in Barthes, as I shall hope to bring out, but it is easy to lose sight of it when there is also so much attractive novelty. Barthes is determined to keep his mind moving, and not to allow his miscellaneous insights and projects for the interpretation of literary texts to harden conveniently into a doctrine.

It seems that he will do anything to avoid definition. '. . . He is intolerant of any *image* of himself, he suffers at being named': that, although it is written in the third person, is what he says of himself in his unusual book of autobiography, *Roland Barthes by Roland Barthes* (1975). What he is fighting against is the idea that he must become an object of attention, for objects are as good as dead—they are known, fixed quantities, without either mystery or the potential for radical change. French intellectuals at least would find this a familiar phobia because it was very much part of postwar existentialism, the philosophical movement which was so widely influential in France between 1945 and the late 1950s.

Barthes, born in 1915, was in fact thirty years old by the end of the Second World War, but he had suffered from consumption and spent much time, especially between 1942 and 1947, in sanatoria, so that his intellectual development was late. Sartrean existentialism marked him profoundly and traces of it have remained, notably in the extreme distaste which Barthes has expressed over and over again for the philosophy to which existentialism was opposed: that of essentialism. Essentialism holds that within each human individual there is some ultimate essence which does not change and which obliges us to behave, as our lives unfold, within more or less predictable limits. It is a philosophy of determinism. Existentialism, on the contrary, preaches the total freedom of the individual constantly to change, to escape determination by his past or any final definition by others. Existence precedes Essence, in the formula of Sartre: not until we are actually dead need we solidify into an essence. Barthes, like Sartre, pits therefore the fluidity, the anarchy even, of existence against the rigor mortis of essentialism; not least because, again following Sartre, he sees essentialism as the ideology which sustains that traditional bugbear of all French intellectuals, the bourgeoisie. Essences and Balances[1] are 'like the zodiacal signs of the bourgeois universe', he writes at the conclusion of his most ferociously anti-bourgeois book, the devastating *Mythologies* (1957).

In one way Barthes goes beyond Sartre in his abhorrence of essentialism. Sartre, so far as one can see, allows the human person a certain integrity or unity; but Barthes professes a philosophy of disintegration, whereby the presumed unity of any individual is dissolved into a plurality and we each of us turn out to be many instead of one. Barthes will have no truck with oneness, and certainly not with God, the One of Ones: he supports whatever is plural or discontinuous. Thus biography is especially offensive to him as a literary form because it represents a counterfeit integration of its subject. It is a false memorial to a living person because it is logical and necessarily centripetal; and that, for Barthes, means that it is untrue to life. His book on *Sade, Fourier, Loyola* (1971) ends

[1] He objects to Balances because they too serve to immobilize the mind. The bourgeois mentality, for Barthes, is adept at finding counterweights for the ideas or phenomena which might otherwise disturb it, and thereby nullifying them. He dislikes such mental equilibrium.

with brief sections called 'Life of Sade' and 'Life of Fourier' which mock at the conventions of literary biography. Fourier's 'life', for instance, is no more than a dozen apparently random facts or impressions numbered from 1 to 12. This is how Barthes fulfils his promise earlier in the book to make of his authors a 'simple plural of charms'. And in the same way he claims to look forward, like a good Epicurean, to his own posthumous dissolution into, on the one hand, elements of matter, and, on the other, scattered memories ('charms') in the minds of his surviving friends. Such will be Nature's endorsement of his deep scepticism towards human identity.

This unusual preference for the plural and centrifugal, as against the singular and coherent, has come to mark Barthes's published work more and more strongly. It is not a fashionable belief—though more fashionable in these generally materialist times than it used to be—nor an altogether persuasive one; since whoever holds it as adamantly as Barthes does risks achieving definition by others as the champion of indefinacy. It is a belief intended by Barthes to contradict what he takes to be more orthodox beliefs in the matter of identity: a paradox, in the old sense of that word, meaning an opinion which runs counter to the accepted wisdom of the age. But paradox has always been Barthes's stock-in-trade. He has seen his vocation, from the outset of his life as a writer, as being antithetical: his arch enemy is the *doxa*, the prevailing view of things, which very often prevails to the extent that people are unaware it is only one of several possible alternative views. Barthes may not be able to destroy the *doxa* but he can lesson its authority by localizing it, by subjugating it to a paradox of his own. So given to paradox is he, indeed, that he is even capable of rounding on his own earlier opinions and denying them.

Barthes is only fully to be appreciated, then, as someone who set out to disrupt as profoundly as he could the orthodox views of literature he found in France when he was a young man. Those views were the ones tenaciously held by university teachers of literature, and it was as the scourge of academic criticism that Barthes first made his name. He had the advantage of not being himself a university teacher of literature; indeed, although he has ended up as a professor in the Collège de France, he has never had an ordinary teaching job in a French university, and this marginal existence—in such institutions as the École Pratique des Hautes Études in Paris—has given him both the freedom and the incentive to work out an independent theory of literature, a theory which attempts, often with great subtlety and realism, to bridge the gap that has traditionally lain open between the academic study of literature and the actual practice of writing.

The grievances against contemporary criticism with which Barthes began were deeply influential on what he came to write later. There were four main ones. First, he objected that literary criticism was predominantly ahistorical, working as it did on the assumption that the moral and formal values of the texts it studied were timeless, and in no way dependent on the nature of the society in which those texts had first been written, published, and read. This was a straightforward Marxist or—since Barthes was never a member of the Communist Party—let us say neo-Marxist objection. He dismissed existing histories of French literature as meaningless chronicles of names and dates: positivistic history of the stalest kind. Literary historians had not begun to grasp that the study of history proper had changed, that by adopting the methods of such great historians as Lucien Febvre they might begin to understand what Barthes calls 'la fonction littéraire' (*On Racine*, 1963). By this he means the role which literature played in any given society: what classes of people wrote books, what classes of people bought them, and so on. A literary history of this kind would work from economic and social facts towards more purely literary ones, and could try to grasp the dialectical relationship between a literature and the society which produced it, or between one literary period and the next.

Barthes's own first published book or essay, *Writing Degree Zero* (1953), was written in order to show what a modern, *marxisant* history of French literature might be like. It is an interesting book but hardly a successful one, partly because it is far too short to do the job Barthes was asking of it. It traces, summarily, the emergence and eventual break-up of an *'écriture bourgeoise'*, which is the description Barthes gives of what others would have called French Classicism. The Classical period of Barthes is the age of bourgeois ascendancy; it was preceded, rather strangely, by nothing, since before about 1650 'French literature had not yet got beyond a problematics of language', and succeeded, round about the middle of the nineteenth century, by a 'crisis', when the bourgeois hegemony collapsed and, instead of just one *écriture*, writers were faced by a choice of *écritures*, every one of which was in its different way 'an act of historical solidarity'. To adopt one *écriture* rather than another required one of those heroic acts of *engagement* or 'commitment' beloved of Sartre and the Existentialists. Those who would avoid such a heavy responsibility sought the way out of a 'blank' or 'neutral' *écriture*—Camus is the example Barthes gives, a writer who by this time had broken with his former left-wing associate, Sartre—which was so utterly impersonal that it seemed to have no historical determinants at all. But this, of course, was an illusion, it was supremely historical.

As polemic *Writing Degree Zero* is an invigorating book and it at once gave Barthes, for all the Sartrean echoes to be heard in it, a distinctive place on the literary left. But it is not always an easy book to understand and some of the crucial concepts which Barthes introduces remain shadowy. This is the case with the term *écriture*, which does not, at this stage, mean at all what it has come to mean in Barthes's mature writings. In *Writing Degree Zero* he appears to use it where other writers would have used the term *style*; certainly he fails to establish what, apart from his own literary intuition, the criteria might be for distinguishing one *écriture* from another, and whether it is legitimate to group all French writers between the years 1650 and 1850 so neatly together as practitioners of the *écriture bourgeoise*.

Barthes's second complaint against academic criticism was that it was psychologically naïve and deterministic. It operated with a model of the human personality made obsolete by the discoveries of psychoanalysis. This naïvety and determinism were pernicious, Barthes argued, when critics chose to explain textual data by biographical ones, or the work by the life—a technique by no means exclusive to French critics nor one as yet eradicated in any country. The elements of a literary work—and this is an absolutely central point in literary structuralism—must be understood in the first instance in their relationship to other elements of that work, and not referred to some context outside literature altogether. 'The homologue of Orestes [in Racine's tragedy of *Andromaque*] is not Racine, it is Pyrrhus [another character in the same play]; that of

Charlus [in Proust's *A la recherche du temps perdu*] is not Montes-quiou,[2] it is the narrator, precisely in so far as the narrator is *not* Proust' (*Critical Essays*, 1964). Moreover, when critics make infer-ences about an author's life from his books they do so blindly, supposing that psychological facts in the work are a direct rep-resentation of psychological facts in the life. This, says Barthes, is quite contradicted by the elementary truths of psychoanalysis, which has shown us that the connection between the two sets of facts is less simple, that 'a desire, a passion, a frustration may very well produce *exactly* contrary representations; a real motive may be *inverted* into an alibi which contradicts it; a work may be the very phantasm which compensates for the negative life . . .' (ibid.).

Barthes breaks with misleading procedures of this kind right at the start of his second book, *Michelet par lui-même* (1954), an anthol-ogy of the writings of that remarkable, highly Romantic nineteenth-century historian, together with Barthes's idiosyncra-tic and ambitious commentary on them. Barthes opens with the warning that 'In this little book the reader will not find either a history of Michelet's ideas, or a history of his life, still less an explanation of one by the other.' This seemingly definitive isola-tion of the text from its author yet goes, in Barthes, with the conviction that a psychoanalytical interpretation of literature is extremely fruitful. But his *Michelet* shows how it is possible to psychoanalyse a text—uncover, that is, its obsessions, its most potent and persistent sexual imagery, its evasions, and so forth—without at the same time believing that you have psychoanalysed its author. Barthes respects the extreme ambiguity of the relationship between an author and what he writes.

His third objection to the academic critics was that they suffered as a race from what he termed 'a-symbolia'. They could see only one meaning in the texts they concerned themselves with, and that one meaning was usually a very literal one. This they subsequently held to be *the* meaning of the text, and that to search further for supplementary or alternative meanings was futile. They were men of narrow and autocratic temper who fancied they were being

---

[2] The Comte Robert de Montesquiou, a rich socialite and aesthetic dabbler of Proust's acquaintance, is remembered now as the 'original' of the character of the Baron de Charlus in Proust's novel.

scientific when they were merely being culpably dogmatic. Their minds were closed to the ambiguities of language, to the coexistence of various meanings within a single form of words, i.e., to symbolism. Here Barthes breaks with the past, and with *Writing Degree Zero*, in so far as he is divorcing the literary work from the circumstances of its production. Literature is ambiguous by definition:

The work is not surrounded, nor designated, nor protected, nor directed by any situation, no practical life is there to tell us what meaning we must give it . . . however prolix it may be, it possesses something of the concision of the Delphic oracle, its words conforming to a first code (the Oracle did not ramble) and yet open to several meanings, because they were uttered outside *any* situation—except the situation of ambiguity itself. . . .

(*Critique et vérité*, 1966)[3]

The critics whose interpretations fail to account for the symbolism inherent in a literary use of language are less than oracular, therefore, and insufficiently pluralist. Even if they can be brought to see more than one meaning in a particular text or passage they will be inclined to keep one and discard the other. They believe in 'right' and 'wrong' meanings. Barthes rejects normative criticism of any kind, arguing that the more meanings a text contains the better, and that no one meaning should be granted precedence over others. He argues also that meaning *pervades* a text, that it is not some final revelation which we get only once we have finished reading it. The difference can best be expressed grammatically: where critics ordinarily invoke *the* or *a* meaning for a work of literature, Barthes invokes the partitive *du sens*, or as we would have to say in English, 'meaning'. And at the same time he shifts the critic's responsibility in respect of meaning by attending not to the product but to the system whereby it is produced: not to significance but to the process of signification. Barthes would like us to understand *how* texts mean before we start worrying about *what* they mean.

His fourth and final criticism of traditional critics was that they never declared publicly what their ideology was, in many cases never even admitted that their criticism *was* ideological. In the Sartrean jargon of the day, they failed to 'assume' the values which

[3] The translations from Barthes's work in this essay are my own.

they applied whenever they pronounced on a literary work. One of the imperatives of Existentialism was that its followers should take full responsibility for their values by making them explicit; to act otherwise was to act in bad faith. But the ideology of positivism, which Barthes saw as pervasive in academic life, remained tacit; and in this way the positivists were able to give the illusion that their values were universal ones, beyond challenge, not the values of a given class in a given society at a given moment of its history. Their bad faith was total.

This was 'mystification', a term of censure which Barthes took over from Marxism and which has been ever since a vital constituent of his vocabulary. Mystification is a sinister, conspiratorial force, whose quite immoral purpose is to endow historical or cultural phenomena with all the appearance of natural ones. The answer to mystification can only be de-mystification, a hygiene which is the responsibility of those members of a community intelligent enough not to be taken in by the mystifiers. Demystification works by demonstrating to the victims of mystification the devious methods by which they have been tricked; it is a technique of social and political enlightenment.

There is an early example of Barthes's own commitment to demystification in *Writing Degree Zero*, where he picks on that most prized of all intellectual values in France, *la clarté*, or lucidity. This, it is widely supposed, is a virtue somehow inherent in the French language which all must recognize; it is a fact of nature requiring no justification. But not in Barthes's reading of the matter. He *locates* this supposedly universal virtue in a society, the society of seventeenth-century France. First *la clarté* was the recommended usage of the French language at court: that is to say, the *écriture* of a small, privileged group of people, Then it was falsely universalized through such agencies as the Port-Royal grammarians, who mistook their own French idiom for the paradigm of human language as a whole. In fact, writes Barthes, *la clarté* is both a local and a political value: '[it] is a purely rhetorical attribute, it is not a general quality of language, possible in all times and in all places, but only the ideal appendix of a certain discourse, that discourse which is subject to a permanent intention of persuasion.' In short, *la clarté* is effective where rhetoric was once effective, in the law courts and perhaps on the hustings; it is a quality of language directed at the shaping of opinion and, in Barthes's conclusive phrase, 'a class idiom'.

These, then, are the four fundamental points at which Barthes distinguished his own conception and practice of criticism from the admittedly narrow-minded criticism which then dominated the literature faculties of French universities. That criticism was never, I trust, as smug or conservative as Barthes pretended it was. Nevertheless, his attacks on it were influential. His work, together with that of other outsiders like him, eventually formed part of what was known for a time as *la Nouvelle Critique*, or the New Criticism. This was a slogan rather than a close association of like-minded innovators, but the mere application of the label was a proof that the point was made, that there was more than one form of literary criticism, that the positivists would have in future to justify their methods rather than merely impose them.

Barthes is no longer the implacable, highly political writer he was when he began; but he is still a committedly paradoxical one. The *doxa*, he writes in *Roland Barthes by Roland Barthes*, 'is the voice of the natural', and it is against the voice of the natural that his own voice has been raised most angrily and brilliantly. His complaint against it, as we have just seen, is that it alienates people, in the Marxist sense of that word. Whatever is taken to be natural is taken to be ordained by some force other than the human. The ultimate alienation occurs when the population of a country is deluded by its ruling class into believing that the social arrangements they live by are not a human product but the product of God or Nature. The power of people to question and transform their institutions has been stolen from them: the eminently changeable has been secured in the interests of a particular group by being disguised as the necessarily permanent. The voice of the natural is a voice in favour of the *status quo*.

To expose it might therefore be held to be a revolutionary act, or at least an act of incitement against the existing constitution of society. But it cannot seriously be said that Barthes, intrepid demystifier though he may have been, was ever a revolutionary. There is much contempt for the bourgeoisie in his earlier writings, but no calls for their heads. He is a man of peace and, increasingly with the years, a man of ecumenicism, prepared to find his deepest pleasures in the coexistence of incompatible views rather than in the extermination of one view by the other. Barthes was always more exercised by cultural than by more nakedly political exploitation, and attracted by demystification for its own sake, as an intellectual pleasure, rather than as a stimulus to violent political action.

Society is a spectacle he can help to explain, by revealing to us some of the mechanisms by which it obscures its artificiality. As a student of Classical Literature at the Sorbonne in the 1930s Barthes was especially involved in the staging of Greek drama, and the lesson of the extreme conventionality of that form was not lost on him. Later, when he started writing, a marked influence on him was the work of the playwright Bertolt Brecht, who unquestionably did look for political revolution to follow on from the preliminary demystification of society by left-wing intellectuals. Barthes shared to the full Brecht's belief in the contemporary need for a drama which *explained* society to people and did not merely represent it. And like Brecht he thought it more effective to make theatre audiences think than to make them feel. He admired the way in which the German writer brought out so aggressively in his plays the inescapably conventional nature of all theatrical performances. This was to undermine the old Romantic illusionism, the idea that the highest art conceals art in the hope of being mistaken for reality.

Nothing could be more Brechtian than the first—and almost certainly most admired—essay in Barthes's *Mythologies*, his major work of cultural demystification. This is the wittiest and most scathing of all his books: to read it is to lose for ever one's innocence towards the ideology that is implicit in the least manifestation of the culture one lives amidst. Barthes's method is to seize on some apparently innocent or ideologically neutral item, such as guidebooks, the Tour de France cycle race, or astrology, and bring out the surreptitious morality that it embodies. He starts with a memorable analysis of the sport of all-in wrestling, a predominantly working-class enthusiasm be it noted, and one regularly condemned in the name of an assumedly universal notion of 'sport' as being no sport at all but 'phoney', because the outcome of each contest has been fixed in advance. Barthes demonstrates the prejudice in that dour 'Jansenist' view and likens all-in wrestling to a classical ritual. It is both a spectacle and excessive, in the sense that the movements and antagonisms of the wrestlers are quite unambiguous; and 'This emphasis is nothing other than the popular and ancestral image of the perfect intelligibility of the real.' In daily life the signs which the world presents to us are wholly ambiguous, their meanings are many and uncertain; but for the space of an hour or two, and within the confines of the wrestling ring, the signs are utterly unequivocal.

This essay stands very suitably at the head of Barthes's substantial collection because it analyses an example of the very kind of spectacle which Barthes himself will offer us: the spectacle of intelligibility. For an hour or two, and within the confines of the book *Mythologies*, the ambiguities of daily life are removed. Barthes, the antagonist of the *doxa*, makes clear to us the obscure stratagems of mystification by his own very emphatic gestures. The 'myth' is another word for the *doxa*, a common, unexamined assumption rooted, as Barthes can show, in the prevailing political order. The bourgeoisie is the villain of *Mythologies*. If Gaston Dominici is condemned to the guillotine (Dominici was a Provençal farmer convicted of murdering an English family; his guilt was not certain and he was not in fact executed), it is because the law courts operate with a bourgeois conception of human psychology derived largely from literature which is not applicable to a peasant such as Dominici and cannot in fact understand him; if the extra-terrestrial creatures who pilot flying saucers are imagined as sharing many of the characteristics of middle-class Frenchmen, this is because 'one of the constant features of petty-bourgeois mythology is this incapacity to imagine the Other' (some of us might want to say that this is an incapacity of the human mind as such, but *Mythologies* is all the more readable a book for being so biased).

It ends with a long theoretical essay called 'The Myth Today' in which Barthes puts forward a method for 'reading' myths of the sort he has been concerned with. The method derives from his experience as a mythographer, rather than the other way round. It derives also from linguistics or, more accurately, from semiotics, the study of sign systems and of signification. It is not too technical, involving little more than an alertness on the part of the student of myths to the difference between the *de*notation of a sign and its *con*notation(s). The denotation is the literal meaning, the connotation the mythical meaning: for the sake of argument connotation can be classified as a symbolism, since connotations are, as it were, additional meanings present along with the literal meaning of the sign in question.

One of Barthes's own examples can serve again here. The sign is a magazine illustration: a coloured soldier in uniform is saluting the French flag. Now it would be possible—possible but absurdly simple-minded—to take this picture at what is conveniently called its 'face value': as a complex of shapes and colours whose signified is the description of the image I have given above; in many cases, though not all, the caption printed underneath such an illustration can be taken as its literal meaning. So far there is no evidence of mythology; but Barthes at once passes beyond the literal meaning to ask what the meaning of the picture as a whole is, appearing where and when it did. It is the front page of *Paris-Match* which now becomes the signifier, and not the various components of the picture which were the original signifiers. What is the signified of this new signifier? The answer, according to Barthes, is French 'imperiality': that is the name he gives to what he interprets as the connotation of the image.

A historical context is needed for an interpretation of this kind. The picture appeared during the time when the French colonial empire was breaking up and when, especially, there was a passionate division of opinion within France as to whether the colony of Algeria should be given its independence. The picture argues tacitly for colonialism. The coloured soldier is assimilated to a white one, whose loyalty to the tricolour he shares. He is the innocent bearer of what for Barthes is a contemptible message: 'that France is a great Empire, that all her sons, without distinction of colour, serve faithfully beneath her flag, and that there is no better answer to the detractors of a supposed colonialism, than the zeal of this Negro to serve his supposed oppressors.'

The example is a good one: Barthes's reading of this particular picture is not fanciful, and it is prejudicial only incidentally, in the sense that a convinced imperialist would find something to admire in the way the message had been silently communicated. It would be reasonable to dislike or to disagree with some of Barthes's cultural 'readings' in *Mythologies*, but there can be no denying that the kind of symbolism in which that book deals is pervasive; that the mass media, to cite the most blatant example, are an inexhaustible source of unstated connotations. The 'mythologue' is the person who will educate us so that we can detect them; he will replace a 'natural' culture with an 'explicative' one. In his role, therefore, as mythologue Barthes is extending the traditional responsibilities of the intellectual in French society in an interesting and very useful direction. The long methodological annexe with which *Mythologies* ends is surely meant didactically, to make more sceptical and aware citizens of us all. From being sheepish consumers of myths Barthes would convert us into cynical readers of them, able if the need arises to re-produce them for ourselves.

The myth, Barthes writes in 'The Myth Today', 'is constituted by the loss of the historical quality of things: in it things lose the memory of their fabrication.' And it is in this concern with fabrication that the mythologue Barthes converges with the literary thinker. Like others of his generation in France, he will not study literary works in isolation from their mode of production. The terminology, yet again, owes a lot to Marxism. Works of literature are *works*, they can be likened to the product of any other place of manufacture (although, curiously, in the industrial world the 'works' is the *place* where things are made, not the things themselves); they are an end-product. The composition of a literary work—the way in which it is made, that is—is of the first importance to a structuralist critic. If it is left out of account, we have mystification, because the work is taken as a finished, natural whole, the product of magic and inspiration rather than intellectual labour.

It is the unholy alliance of Romanticism and Realism which is to blame for a certain school of criticism's failure to appreciate that writing too is work. Romanticism likes to economize on effort and to gloss over the fatigue of composition, maintaining that those who create literature are superior and original souls not to be confused with lower sorts of labourer. Realism understands writing to be the representation of something which is already there before the writer sets to work, that something being either reality as such or else the notions of reality stored in the writer's head. Barthes will have no truck with precepts such as these.

They add up, he suggests, to a crude misrepresentation of what literature is—failing, for one thing, to distinguish the literary from the non-literary. This distinction, the establishment of which has been one of the largest ambitions of twentieth-century Formalism, is a question of language; it is a distinction also which nineteenth-century Realism suppressed. Realism is an enemy for Barthes, as it has been for other modern theorists, because it is anti-art. It makes of literature the servant of reality because it holds an instrumental view of language; Realism presupposes that language is transparent, as it were, that 'through' words we look at life. Realism stresses signifieds at the expense of signifiers and teaches that, in the actual practice of writing, meanings precede sounds. The words which a writer employs will have been determined in advance by the meaning he wishes to convey, with the result that, provided he knows his craft, his language will be both purposeful and unambiguous.

Much use of language, Barthes allows, is of this kind: the writer has an objective and arranges words in order to achieve it. He wishes to inform or instruct his readers. But that can never be a specifically literary use of language. Literature does not inform or instruct in this drably pragmatic way; it delivers language from the constraints which in daily life confine it to the more mechanical role of an instrument. Literary language is, by comparison, purposeless, and when we read it we are not being asked to *do* anything as a direct result.

In an essay of 1960 called 'Écrivains et écrivants' (reprinted in *Critical Essays*), Barthes made a dramatic qualitative distinction between two sorts of writer. The first, and lesser, sort is the *écrivant*, for whom language is the means to some extra-linguistic end. He is a transitive writer in that he has a direct object. He intends that whatever he writes should carry one meaning only, the meaning he himself wants to transmit to his readers. The *écrivain* is a nobler, more auspicious figure by far, 'priestly' where the *écrivant* is merely 'clerical', to use one of Barthes's own antitheses (and this resurrection of the old notion of the writer as someone akin to a priest is an indication of Barthes's own underlying romanticism). The *écrivain* writes intransitively in so far as he devotes his attention to the means—which is language—instead of the end, or the meaning. He is preoccupied by words not by the world:

The *écrivain* fulfils a function, the *écrivant* an activity, that much we learn from grammar, which rightly opposes the substantive of the one to the (transitive) verb of the other. Not that the *écrivain* is a pure essence: he acts, but his action is immanent to its object, it is exercised, paradoxically, on its own instrument: language; the *écrivain* is someone who *works* on his language (even if inspired) and is functionally absorbed into that work. The activity of the *écrivain* involves two types of norm: technical ones (of composition, genre, writing) and artisanal ones (of work, patience, correcting, perfecting). The paradox is that, the raw material having become in some ways its own end, literature is basically a tautological activity . . . the *écrivain* is one who absorbs the *why* of the world radically into a *how to write*. And the miracle, if we can put it like that, is that all through the literary ages this narcissistic activity has not ceased to pose a question to the world. . . .

This distinction between the *écrivain* and the *écrivant* is one which Barthes has continued to build on, even though that particular pair of contrasted terms quickly dropped out of his writing. Like others of the pairs of terms that he has introduced since, they are to be understood hypothetically: real writers, as Barthes acknowledges, will be a mixture of *écrivain* and *écrivant*, sometimes the priest and sometimes the clerk, sometimes conveying a predetermined meaning and sometimes playing with language to see what emerges.

It is the *écrivain* who is of interest because he is, in Barthes's prophetic scheme, the writer of the future. The literary world may hardly be ready for him yet, even in avant-garde Paris, but his time will come—or so at least Barthes seems to promise. He is not, as one might at first think, a throwback to Romanticism and to that happily dilapidated critical edifice, the Ivory Tower. The *écrivain* is withdrawn but he is no dreamer; rather, he is a toiling language-worker whose isolation lasts only for as long as he is actually writing and who, far from washing his hands of the world, is its conscience, since his duty is to sound out his native language to the full.

The *écrivain* does not work *from* meanings, as the *écrivant* does, he works *towards* them. As Barthes likes to put it, meaning is 'postponed'. It is there, as it should be, when eventually we come to read what he has written: 'the *écrivain* conceives literature as an end, the world returns it to him as a means'. The world is ourselves and we read literature instrumentally, as if it were the work of an *écrivant*. We assume the process of signification has travelled from signified to signifier: the writer knew what he wanted to say, then he decided how exactly he should say it. We are upset if we are asked to believe the opposite, that an author had first decided how to say and only then discovered what 'it' was; this reversal of our habits seems degrading to the whole notion of authorship. But Barthes could claim that his version of how signification works is frequently true to the facts.[4] It has the enormous merit of not positing, as the alternative version does, immaterial signifieds which somehow exist in the writer's mind even before signifiers are found for them.

The *écrivain* is obedient to the defiant injunction of Mallarmé, to 'cede the initiative to words'. He is the paradoxical hero of structuralism: the creature of the system, in this instance of language. No longer is the author to be seen as a Subject full of conscious but as yet private meanings who will take advantage of language to make them public. That model of authorship is for Barthes a fossil, dating back to the days of essentialist psychology; it should never have survived the discoveries made in this century about the limitations on the autonomy of the Ego. The model with which Barthes would replace it is more in keeping with the times, being patronized more or less equally by Marx and by Freud, those two supreme shapers of the contemporary French mind. The *écrivain* is first of all a materialist and, as we have seen, a worker; he works with the materiality of language, with its signifiers. The signifiers and signifieds of a language are to be seen as its infrastructure and superstructure, as in the classical Marxian analysis of society; and change comes from below, from tinkering with the signifiers. (The *écrivant*, for whom the signifieds come first, is of course that shameful person, an Idealist.) One can see the appeal of an analogy such as this, to left-wing French intellectuals traditionally guilty about the economic and intellectual gulf that exists between themselves and the proletariat they champion; but language-workers are workers only in an honorary sense and have a flimsy title to this enrolment into the materialist cause. What we might concede to Barthes is that a philosophical materialist—and not all philosophical materialists are Marxists by any means—ought, to be

[4] Cf. the old 'paradox': 'How do I know what I mean till I see what I say'.

logical, to write materialistically: he ought to become an *écrivain*.[5]

The Freudian influence on Barthes's model of the writer is less figurative, and equally materialist. It showed as far back as *Writing Degree Zero*, where he defines what in those days he was prepared to call the 'style' of a writer. Style lies almost beyond literature:

Images, a delivery, a lexicon are born of the writer's body and his past and gradually become the very automatisms of his art. Thus, under the name of style, an autarchic language takes shape which plunges only into the personal and secret mythology of the author, into that hypophysics of the word [*parole*], where the first couplet of words and things is formed, and where the great verbal themes of his existence are established once and for all.

Barthes has seldom since discussed style as such, but he has not abandoned the view that when we write we write in part to the dictation of our bodies. Indeed, if we fail to do so we cannot write authentically at all:

The stereotype is that emplacement in discourse *where the body is lacking*, when one is sure that it is not. Inversely, in this supposedly collective text I am in the middle of reading, occasionally the stereotype (the *écrivance*) gives way and writing [*l'écriture*] appears; I am sure then that this brief utterance has been produced by *a* body.

(*Roland Barthes by Roland Barthes*; Barthes's own italics)

And elsewhere in the same book, writing of the *doxa* and of repetition in general, Barthes excepts from blame the repetition 'which comes from the body'.

He has chosen the word 'body' to describe the source of these vital and characteristic determinants of a writer's language where others might have used 'the subconscious'. What comes from the 'body' does not come from the mind: Barthes's metaphor is a striking and a logical one. In pre-Freudian days, the writer's self could be conceived of as a sort of shock-proof kernel, standing above and outside language; but now it has become much more a plaything of language, for as soon as the writer sits down to write he is dislocated and transformed by what Barthes also calls 'verbal pulsations'. These are the voice either of his 'body', his psychic

[5] In Barthes's terms, Social Realism, so much favoured by official Marxist writers, is a thoroughly Idealist mode of writing because it uses language purely instrumentally.

case-history so to speak, or of language itself—those unsolicited associations of signifiers to which we are all of us subject. And in *A Lover's Discourse* (1977) Barthes goes further than ever before in the overt Freudianization of the writer's work by tracing the birth of language in the human infant to the desire to 'manipulate the absence' of its mother. This would make the activity of the *écrivain* a re-enactment of a peculiarly distressing primal scene, since the writer, unlike the speaker of language, writes in isolation and addresses only phantasmal interlocutors, never real ones.

Among the ancestors of the *écrivain*, then, we can number the Surrealists, who in the practice of 'automatic writing' also invited their bodies to speak for them. However, we should pass on now from the process of writing to the product. Just as the intentions and activity of *écrivain* and *écrivant* are at variance, so are the goods they produce. The *écrivain* produces a Text, the *écrivant* only a Work. As before, it is the Text which matters, and as before the Text is still a hypothesis, a possibility for the future and at the same time a standard against which to measure the Works of the past and present. The Text is a sort of verbal carnival, in which language is manifestly out on parole from its humdrum daily tasks. The writer's language-work results in a linguistic spectacle, and the reader is required to enjoy that spectacle for its own sake rather than to look through language to the world. A Text comes, in fact, from consorting with the signifiers and letting the signifieds take care of themselves; it is the poetry of prose.

The nearest we have to a genuine Text is James Joyce's *Finnegans Wake*, a book that has known a small vogue in France as a result of Barthes's theorizing. *Finnegans Wake* has generally been classed with our literature's noble aberrations; our habits of reading are formed on Works and this Text is too much for them. We tire easily of it, or deplore it as meaningless. But far from being meaningless, *Finnegans Wake* is the most consciously and inventively meaningful book in the language; it is the lack of a single, over-all meaning which worries us. It must be taken word by word and sentence by sentence, the meanings proliferating as we go. *Finnegans Wake* is Textual, in Barthes's terms, and altogether desirable, in that it disperses our minds instead of concentrating them. It lacks finality and whatever lacks finality is for Barthes a good. There is—he is right—something austere about waiting until the end of a book for our satisfaction; the *continuous* satisfaction that he asks of a Text testifies to his own ineradicable hedonism as a reader or critic of literature.

It is one of the virtues of the lover in *A Lover's Discourse* that he too is 'withdrawn from all finality'. He is the spokesman of a logic different from the world's logic:

I am simultaneously and contradictorily both happy and unhappy: 'to succeed' or 'to fail' have for me only ephemeral, contingent meanings (this does not stop my desires and sorrows from being violent ones); what impels me, secretly and obstinately, is not tactical: I accept and I affirm, irrespective of the true and the false, of success and failure; I am withdrawn from all finality, I live according to chance. . . .

Barthes's lover resists any helpful or sympathetic suggestion for possible resolutions of his plight, because to look forward to its end would be to lessen its immediacy . He does not want it to have a 'sense', remembering that the French word *sens* means both 'sense' and 'direction'. The *Lover's Discourse* is a melancholy book to read because the state of being in love is presented by Barthes as a very painful one; but against the pain must be set the lover's perverse pleasure at finding himself trapped in a perfectly intractable situation. The very form that Barthes has given the book conspires against any idea of there being some teleological force at work that might be the light at the end of the lover's tunnel. The arrangement of its contents—of what Barthes calls the 'figures' of the lover's discourse—is alphabetical; which is the most impersonal arrangement of all. What Barthes has carefully avoided is any suggestion of a narrative element to the book, of an *histoire d'amour*; the form of the *Discourse* is as it is so as to 'discourage the temptation of meaning [*sens*]'.

And as with the love affair, so with the Text. Neither leads anywhere, both are charged uninterruptedly with an intense meaning. The lover finds himself, in another emphatic phrase from the *Lover's Discourse*, 'in the brazier of meaning', because of his compulsive need to interpret the ambiguous signs of the Loved One's behaviour. The lover is thus also a reader. But he is a reader of a particular kind, the kind that a Text, composed by a true *écrivain*, deserves. What he is attempting to do is to understand that

Text from within, to re-produce it for himself. He is far too emotional, as someone in love, passively to settle for it as a mere
representation of the Loved One.

The Text which the Loved One weaves counts, unless I am
mistaken (Barthes himself makes no such connection), as a *scriptible* one, the *scriptible* being a Text so written as to make of its
readers producers instead of consumers. They are *scriptible*, or
'writable', because the reader as it were re-writes them as he reads,
having been induced to mimic in his own mind the process by
which the Text came to be written in the first place. Texts are
scriptible by definition; Works on the other hand, and that means all
the literature we have experience of, are *lisible*, or 'readable'. We do
not rewrite those, we simply read them; and read them moreover
from start to finish, since Works *are* teleological, they move
towards an appointed end. We proceed horizontally through a
Work, but vertically, if that is possible, through a Text—the
ultimate in Texts, I fancy, would be a single, infinitely meaningful
word, which we could use as the dispensable cue for our own
language-work.

The concept of the *scriptible* is an exotic one, but not quite as
far-fetched as one might at first think. There is at least a partial
justification of it in, for example, the derivations which Proust
reports as having made from a number of proper nouns by breaking them into syllables and then pondering the associations which
these now meaningless sounds had for him. This is surely a very
Textual procedure. Indeed, in *The Pleasure of the Text* (1973),
Barthes speaks of the Text as 'undoing nomination'. What he has
in mind is not so much the Proustian dissolution of the *nom* as an
abstention from pronouncing it. As with Mallarmé, the reverbera-
tions are to be preferred to the thing itself. Barthes has made the
point again in an anecdote:

A. confides to me that he couldn't bear it if his mother were promiscuous,
but that he could bear it if his father were; he adds: Strange, isn't it? A
single noun would suffice to put an end to his astonishment: Oedipus! As I
see it, A. is very close to the text, because the text *does not give the nouns* . . .
[Barthes's italics].

The word 'Oedipus' here is the disembodied stereotype, the *doxa*;
its effect, if immediately pronounced, would have been to foreclose

on A.'s Text. And that, if the remarkable theses of *The Pleasure of the Text* be conceded, would be to rob him of his happiness too. For what Barthes seems to claim is that the relationship between writer, Text, and reader is an erotic one. Body speaks unto body; the 'body' of the writer, which is the most real and intimate part of him, is offered to the 'body' of the reader, who responds equally intimately.

But, as always with Barthes, there are two qualitatively distinct modes of response to a Text. There is *plaisir*, or 'pleasure', and there is *jouissance*, or 'enjoyment'. The connotations of *jouissance* in French are sexual, and those connotations are crucial to Barthes's distinction. *Plaisir* is a homely enough feeling, one might even say a bourgeois feeling, appropriate to the fireside and to writing that is *lisible*; *jouissance* on the other hand is extreme and disconcerting, and appropriate to writing that is *scriptible*. No description can be given of it: '*plaisir* is sayable, *jouissance* is not,' affirms Barthes, using an opposition borrowed from psychoanalysis. And again, *jouissance* 'puts us into a state of loss, it discomforts us (to the extent even of a certain boredom), it rocks the reader's historical, cultural and psychological foundations, and the consistency of his tastes and values and memories; it brings about a crisis in his relations with language.'

Few readers will identify this as an experience they have actually had or are ever likely to have from their reading. It is provoked, as far as one can make out from *The Pleasure of the Text*, which is often an elusive book, by the semantic anarchy which is inseparable from the authentic Text and by the flaunting of the author's neuroses (his 'body'). Barthes looks forward to writing which dramatizes above all the conflict between cultural conformism and exuberant subversion: a subversion of the existing forms of language. He calls, almost mystically, for 'a new philosophical state of language-matter'—which will serve as a slogan but hardly as an indication of what he has in mind.

Barthes is a disappointing prophet, but he is prophetic only when he is especially anxious to undermine certain ideological principles, and to show that all principles are transient. His future—where the *écrivains* work at language and eventually inspire *jouissance* with their *scriptible* Texts—is comprehensible only as a stick with which he means to beat the present. And what Barthes appears to find most noxious in that present is its persistent belief in the integrity both of persons and of literary works. (Integrity here is to be taken in a philosophical sense: to mean one-ness.) Works and authors are commonly understood to be entities or wholes; as critical categories they imply essentialism. Barthes began, as we have seen, as an enemy of essentialism and he has remained one; and in his later writings his arguments against it have become both subtler and more complete.

So far as actual works of literature go, those arguments are deployed to the full in *S/Z*, the study which Barthes published in 1970 of a little-known but colourful novella by Balzac. It was by this book that Barthes first began to make his name outside France with others than specialists in French literature, no doubt because it offers reassurance that the oracle is also splendidly capable of being an artisan, and of buckling down to some empirical Lit. Crit. Not that *S/Z* is empirical in any narrow way; it is also speculative, and constitutes an extremely valuable study of the traditional methods of narrative writing as a whole.

Barthes took Balzac as his subject for a reason: that Balzac has traditionally been interpreted as the archetypal Realist, the writer whose aim was to represent early nineteenth-century France in its historical reality. Barthes's intention is to show, by long and careful analysis of the text, how wholly conventional Balzac's method was, and how the Realist above all depended for his inspiration not on life but on art. *S/Z* is an unfair book—the story which Barthes has chosen, *Sarrasine*, is an eccentric one for Balzac, and by no means central to the 'Comédie humaine'—but a telling one.

Barthes's own words in *S/Z* outnumber Balzac's by a good six or seven to one. This degree of unbalance, between text and commentary, is common in the study of poetry, exceedingly rare in the study of prose, for the reason not only that poetry is considered to be a more condensed use of language than prose, but also that, since it is not usually discursive, poetry can be chopped up ready for examination with less detriment to its continuity. As we know, the will to disintegration is unsleeping in Barthes, and his first act with *Sarrasine* is to divide it up into 561 *lexies*, or 'units of reading'. Some of these are only a few words long, others several sentences;

each is the subject of an analysis, some short and others quite extensive. Only once the whole story has been picked over in this way is Balzac's text reunited and printed, a trifle condescendingly perhaps, as an appendix at the end of the volume.

But this ruthless dissolution of the text is only a start; the categories which Barthes introduces in order to conduct his analysis of it are even more destructive of its supposed unity. These are the five codes, which have become one of his most admired innovations. Each has a different responsibility: the Hermeneutic and Actional codes regulate the sequences of events in the story, the first being concerned with the narrative 'enigmas' which the story poses and eventually solves, the second quite straightforwardly with the successive stages into which a distinct action is divided; the Semic and Symbolic codes Barthes uses to catalogue the meanings of characters, situations, and events in the story, the Symbolic code being reserved for the various oppositions on which the narrative structure is founded; and the Referential code, finally, is held to codify all the many references which the story makes to a reality outside the text.

This last code is a controversial one because it is in a text's references to an extra-textual or historical reality that the practice of Realism is held mainly to lie. Barthes introduces the Referential code, provocatively, last of all, and asks it to take care of *Sarrasine's* numerous references to morality, psychology, history, and art. These references one might think were Balzac's own: those points in his story where he introduced his own thoughts and preferences and embedded his fiction solidly in the reality of his time. But not so, according to Barthes, who delights in proving how the arch-realist refers constantly not directly to life but to the common-places of the age, to the *doxa*. The 'real' turns out to be the 'already written'; any originality that might have been claimed for Balzac vanishes before the authority of the code. Balzac is not inventing, he is quoting; he is even accused at one point of 'spewing out stereotypes', a crime which Barthes could never forgive. More damagingly, he points out also how the verbal descriptions of people and places which are so supremely Realist and characteristically Balzacian, themselves originate in the techniques not of writing but of painting:

To describe is thus to set up the empty frame which the realist author transports always with him (more important than his easel), before a collection or continuum of objects that would be inaccessible to the word were it not for this maniacal operation. . . . Thus realism . . . consists, not in copying the real, but in copying a (painted) copy of the real: that famous real . . . is set further back, or deferred, or at least grasped through the pictural dross with which it has been daubed before being subjected to the word: code upon code, says realism.

This is both polemical and perceptive: a fine and complex insight into the twofold conventionality of prose description but not in the end a proof that Realism as it has traditionally been thought of is impossible. The descriptive writer is not picturing, he is writing pictorially; there is a homology between what he does and what a painter does, but that is as far as it goes.

The major injustice of which Barthes is guilty in *S/Z* is the glibness with which he invokes the accepted wisdom of Balzac's own time whenever the Referential code comes into play. Admittedly, Balzac is not famous for his moral or psychological acumen, but that does not mean that he had no insights of his own at all into contemporary human behaviour in France. In point of fact Barthes is referring Balzac's various judgements in *Sarrasine* to a corpus of 'stereotypes' which does not exist. Barthes cannot know, because no one can know, exactly where Balzac is *referring* to current notions of human psychology, let us say, and where he is hoping to amend those notions in order to bring them closer into line with what he believed to be the facts. When Balzac talks of 'the kind of frenzy which only disturbs us at that age when desire has something terrible and infernal about it', Barthes allots this dismissively to 'the psychology of age' as if it were unthinkable that it might be the fruit of observation or experience. Under his dispensation it is hard to see how the common stock of knowledge or belief could ever be modified.

Sarrasine is very much a Work and not a Text: it is *lisible*, not *scriptible*. Nevertheless, in *S/Z* Barthes manages to flood it with meanings. It has what he calls 'a limited plurality'. It is not, by the time he has finished analysing it, and distributing its different elements among his five codes, at all the unity that it was. Its continuity has been broken by the division into *lexies*: or rather its discontinuity has been exposed, since the continuity of a text is a deception. To undeceive us in this respect has been a most important part of Barthes's programme, because the continuum belongs in nature not in art. One of his sharpest criticisms of Michelet is that Michelet preferred the continuous to the discontinuous, that is to say the organic to the analytical. In Michelet, complains Barthes, 'Nature is no longer a catalogue . . . it is a smooth expanse [*une nappe*]', and he has returned a number of times in his books to this idea of the *nappe*, as being the disguise which the artificial wears when it wishes to appear as the natural. The *nappe*, and even more the *nappé*, i.e. whatever has been made to look like a *nappe* (the term comes from cooking, and describes a dish that has had a smooth sauce poured over it), are not to be tolerated. Thus, in *S/Z*, Barthes writes contemptuously of how, in the classical text such as *Sarrasine*, ' "Life" thus becomes a sickening mixture of current opinions, a stifling *nappe* of received ideas.'

And just as the narrative of *Sarrasine* is irremediably broken up, so too is its author. The great aim of *S/Z* is to 'de-originate' the text, to demonstrate in what way it is a weaving together of many voices rather than the utterance of just one—that of Balzac. All texts, even those as thoroughly *lisible* as *Sarrasine*, give voice to a chorus (and the more cacophonous that chorus proves to be the better we should like it, if we are faithful Barthesians). *S/Z* bears out quite dazzlingly the structuralist premise that 'the rule is openly substituted for subjectivity, and technique for expression' (*On Racine*). There is no question of Balzac being thought of as 'expressing himself' in *Sarrasine* because that would be Idealism, which believes that the writer has a self independent of and pre-existing what he writes and that he sets out to represent his self in language. That Barthes does not allow. For him a writer's 'self' is a convention of the text of which he is the author, a 'creature of paper' or else an 'effect of language' (*Roland Barthes by Roland Barthes*).

The writer is thus no more than the grammatical subject, real or implied, of a piece of writing: the explicit or implicit 'I'. He is not a substantive presence to be located, as in the past, 'behind' the text. He has undergone a dissolution because he is to be found everywhere in what he writes. In a text 'the subject comes undone, as if a spider were to dissolve itself into its web' (*The Pleasure of the Text*). The writer therefore dwells in his text as a form; materially speaking, he is a personal pronoun. Much of his reality has had to be sacrificed because language is an objective, collective system which we can only use, never expropriate. The real 'I' is thus debarred from ever putting in an appearance: 'I cannot *write* myself. What is this me that might write itself? As it entered into the writing [*l'écriture*], the writing would deflate it, would make it useless . . .' (*A Lover's Discourse*). When he turns to writing about himself, as in *Roland Barthes by Roland Barthes*, Barthes lives strictly up to his own rules and appears there in the third person, either as 'he' or as 'RB'. In the subsequent *Lover's Discourse*, on the other hand, which is not offered as an autobiographical work although there are self-evidently autobiographical moments in it, he chooses to write in the first person throughout. But this first person is that representative first person which philosophers like to use when they pause to instantiate some abstract argument ('I am sitting in my study. I see a chair. What is actually involved in my seeing a chair?'; and so forth). This is an impersonal, structural 'I', an empty form with which we can each identify.

A text without an author is not an idea most of us are quite prepared for. Our fundamental but often unacknowledged Idealism, Barthes would say, insists that there be a ghost in the textual machine, an immaterial presence of which the text is the outward sign. Barthes would also say that this was a specifically Western view of things, and that other views are possible. In Japan, when he travelled there, he found evidence as he believed of a quite contradictory metaphysic, one of vacancy. In Japanese culture, or at any rate Barthes's version of it, the exterior of a thing *is* the thing, there is no informing but invisible agency within. Japan is a country full of rich and intriguing signifiers whose charm is that they have no signifieds.

Barthes has published a book about Japan called *L'Empire des signes* (1970) which is very much a part of his *œuvre*. In it he considers a variety of Japanese practices: cooking, *bunraku* puppet theatres, gardening, *haiku*, gift-wrapping, and so on. All of them, he finds, exhibit the same 'exemption of the sense'; they are all surface and no hidden depths; they have neither centre nor 'soul'. Take parcels: in the West we incorrigible Idealists like to remove the wrapping as quickly as we can in order to get to the contents; in

Japan it is apparently the wrapping which counts and which is appreciated, whereas the contents may be either utterly trivial or non-existent. Take, even, the Japanese face: in the West, again, our eyes are deep-set and are taken to be signs of the soul within; the Oriental eye, set more or less flush with the surface of the body, invites no such intromission. (One hesitates to call this an insight into the Japanese mind but it is a seductive example of Barthes's passionate consistency of interpretation in *L'Empire des signes*. There is surely a flaw in the argument: the opposition deep-set/flush is itself a Western not a Japanese one, and the Japanese might very well employ a different code in order to locate the Oriental soul.)

The Japan which is analysed in *L'Empire des signes* may or may not answer to the real Japan; certainly it is a culture offering welcome asylum to a refugee like Barthes from the stifling bourgeois Idealism he has all his life detested. He is perhaps entitled to his Japan as an Archimedean lever with which to unseat the West, as the utopian instrument of our disintegration. For there is much of the outsider in Barthes, of the person who willingly alienates himself from the culture in which he lives the better to explain and at the same time to judge it. He has once or twice posed in his time as a 'scientist', bringing what are uncommonly sharp powers of analysis to bear on processes of signification but without revealing any moral or political attitude towards them. These have been the only dull or unsatisfactory moments of his literary career (I am thinking above all of the technical sections of *Système de la mode* (1967), Barthes's long semiotic study of fashion writing). Barthes is not a scientist but a moralist—anyone who has read *A Lover's Discourse* must recognize that.

I do not mean by that that he wants to impose a particular form of morality on other people, because nothing could be further from the truth: he is the patentee after all of a conception of writing which sees it ideally as an activity beyond Good and Evil. He is a moralist in the sense that moral passions and distinctions excite him, and he would like, as the French moralists of the seventeenth century did, to try and plot them on paper. His writings are diverse but underlying them is a philosophical consistency. Barthes is both a materialist in philosophy and an avowed hedonist, judging intellectual experiences, like experience in general, by the gratification they provide.

One of the lessons he has taught is that we have scant right to call our language our own, because it is a system to which we must surrender much of our individuality whenever we enter it. Whoever speaks or writes is, in his description, no more than 'the great empty envelope' around the words. Barthes, the author, may be only the name on an envelope, but no one in recent years has put the French language to richer, more original, or more intelligent use.

Bibliography

Roland Barthes was born in Cherbourg in 1915, and was brought up in Bayonne and Paris. He graduated in Classics from the Sorbonne in 1939. After the war he taught at the Universities of Bucharest and Alexandria and, from 1960, at the École Pratique des Hautes Études in Paris. In 1976 he became Professor of Literary Semiology at the Collège de France.

BOOKS

Le Degré zéro de l'écriture (Paris, 1953); English translation, *Writing Degree Zero* (London, 1967; New York, 1977)

Michelet par lui-même (Paris, 1954)

Mythologies (Paris, 1957); the English translation, *Mythologies* (London, 1972), includes only a selection of the essays in the original.

Sur Racine (Paris, 1963); English translation, *On Racine* (New York, 1964)

Essais critiques (Paris, 1964); English translation, *Critical Essays* (Evanston, Ill., 1972)

Éléments de sémiologie (Paris, 1965); English translation, *Elements of Semiology* (London, 1967; New York, 1977)

Critique et vérité (Paris, 1966)

Système de la mode (Paris, 1967)

S/Z (Paris, 1970); English translation, *S/Z* (New York, 1974; London, 1975)

L'Empire des signes (Geneva, 1970)

Sade, Fourier, Loyola (Paris, 1971); English translation, *Sade, Fourier, Loyola* (New York, 1976; London, 1977)

Nouveaux essais critiques, included with reprint of *Degré zéro de l'écriture* (Paris, 1972)

Le Plaisir du texte (Paris, 1973); English translation, *The Pleasure of the Text* (New York, 1975; London, 1976)

Roland Barthes par Roland Barthes (Paris, 1975); English translation, *Roland Barthes by Roland Barthes* (London and New York, 1977)

Fragments d'un discour amoureux (Paris, 1977); English translation, *A Lover's Discourse: Fragments* (New York, 1978; London, 1979)

Leçon (Paris, 1978)

Sollers Écrivain (Paris, 1979)

A selection of Barthes's many uncollected essays has been published in English translation as *Image–Music–Text*, ed. S. Heath (London, 1977; New York, 1978).

Michel Foucault

HAYDEN WHITE

The work of Michel Foucault, conventionally labelled as structuralist but consistently denied by him to be such, is extraordinarily difficult to deal with in any short account. This is not only because his *œuvre* is so extensive, but also because his thought comes clothed in a rhetoric apparently designed to frustrate summary, paraphrase, economical quotation for illustrative purposes, or translation into traditional critical terminology.

In part, the idiosyncrasy of Foucault's rhetoric reflects a general rebellion of his generation against the *clarté* of their Cartesian heritage. But the thorniness of Foucault's style is also ideologically motivated. His interminable sentences, parentheses, repetitions, neologisms, paradoxes, oxymorons, alternation of analytical with lyrical passages, and his combination of scientistic with mythic terminology—all this appears to be consciously designed to render his discourse impenetrable to any critical technique based on ideological principles different from his own.

It is difficult, however, to specify Foucault's own ideological position. If he detests liberalism because of its equivocation and service to the social *status quo*, he also despises conservatism's dependence on tradition. And although he often joins forces with Marxist radicals over specific causes, he shares nothing of their faith in science. The anarchist left he dismisses as infantile in its hopes for the future and naïve in its faith in a benign human nature. His philosophical position is close to the nihilism of Nietzsche. His discourse begins where Nietzsche's, in *Ecce Homo*, left off: in the perception of the 'madness' of all 'wisdom' and the 'folly' of all 'knowledge'. But there is nothing of Nietzsche's optimism in Foucault. His is a chillingly clear perception of the transiency of all learning, but he draws the implications of this perception in a manner which has nothing in common with Nietzsche's adamantine rigour.

And this because there is no centre to Foucault's discourse. It is all surface—and intended to be so. For even more consistently than Nietzsche, Foucault resists the impulse to seek an origin or transcendental subject which would confer any specific 'meaning' on human life. Foucault's discourse is wilfully superficial. And this is consistent with the larger purpose of a thinker who wishes to dissolve the distinction between surfaces and depths, to show that wherever this distinction arises it is evidence of the play of organized power, and that this distinction is itself the most effective weapon that power possesses for hiding its operations.

The manifold operations of power are, in Foucault's view, at once most manifest and most difficult to identify in what he takes to be the basis of cultural praxis in general, namely discourse. Discourse is the term under which he gathers all of the forms and categories of cultural life, including, apparently, his own efforts to submit this life to criticism. As thus envisaged, and as he himself says in *The Archaeology of Knowledge* (1969), his own work is to be regarded as 'a discourse about discourses'. It follows, then, that if we are to comprehend his work on its own terms, we must analyse it *as* discourse—and with all the connotations of circularity, of movement back and forth, which the Indo-European root of this term (*kers*) and its Latinate form (*dis-*, 'in different directions', + *currere*, 'to run') suggest. Accordingly, I have sought entry into the thicket of Foucault's work and, I hope, a way out of it, by concentrating on its nature as discourse.

My approach will be generally rhetorical and my aim will be to characterize the style of Foucault's discourse. I think we will find a clue to the meaning of his discursive style in the rhetorical theory of tropes, those 'turns' of speech by which language is transformed into poetic utterance. This theory has served as the organizing principle of Foucault's theory of culture, and it will serve as the analytical principle of the essay that follows. Briefly, I argue that the *authority* of Foucault's discourse derives primarily from its style (rather than from its 'factual evidence' or rigour of argument); that this style gives a place of privilege to the trope of catachresis (the misapplication of a word) in its own elaboration; and that, finally, this trope serves as the model of the 'world view' from which Foucault launches his criticisms of humanism, science, 'reason', and most of the institutions of Western culture as they have evolved since the Renaissance.

At the end of *The Archaeology of Knowledge*, Foucault's systematic exposition of the analytical principles informing his earlier studies of madness, clinical medicine, and the human sciences, he states that his intention is 'to free the history of thought from its subjection to transcendence . . . to cleanse it of all transcendental narcissism; [and free it] from [the] circle of the lost origin . . .'. This statement, with its combination of extravagance and obscurity, is typical of Foucault's style and suggests the difficulty of translating his discourse into any other terms. The statement occurs in the course of an imagined exchange between Foucault and his critics (or between two sides of Foucault's own intellectual persona), in which the methods of the structuralists and those of Foucault are juxtaposed and the differences between them clearly marked.

One issue in the exchange hinges on what Foucault takes to be the 'crisis' of Western Culture. This is a crisis

that concerns that transcendental reflection with which philosophy since Kant has identified itself; which concerns the theme of the origin, that promise of the return, by which we avoid the difference of our present; which concerns an anthropological idea that orders all these questions around the question of man's being, and allows us to avoid an analysis of practice; which concerns all humanistic ideologies; which, above all, concerns the status of the subject.

Structuralism seeks to avoid discussion of this crisis, Foucault says, by 'pursuing the pleasant games of genesis and system, synchrony and development, relation and cause, structure and history'. The imagined structuralist (or Foucault's counter-persona) then asks the questions which still remain unanswered in most discussions of Foucault's work: 'What then is the title of your discourse? Where does it come from and from where does it derive its right to speak? How could it be legitimated?'

These are fair questions, even when addressed to a thinker to whom 'fairness' is simply another rule imported from the domain of ethics to set restrictions on the free play of desire; and Foucault's answers to them seem curiously weak. It is to his credit as a serious thinker that he even raises them in his own text, but he takes away in his answers as much as he gives in permitting the questions to be raised. His own discourse, he says (again in *The Archaeology of Knowledge*), 'far from determining the locus in which it speaks, is avoiding the ground on which it could find support.' His discourse 'is trying to operate a decentring that leaves no privilege to any centre . . . it does not set out to be a recollection of the original or a memory of the truth. On the contrary, its task is to *make* differences . . . it is continually making *differentiations*, it is a *diagnosis*.' And he adds, in that constant repetition of 'the same in the different' which is the distinguishing mark of his discourse, 'it is an attempt . . . to show that to speak is to do something—something other than to express what one thinks; to translate what one knows, and something other than to play with the structures of a language [*langue*] . . .'

What this 'something other' may be, however, is more easily defined by what it is *not*, in Foucault's view. And he ends *The Archaeology of Knowledge* with a negative definition of his central object of study in the form of a 'message' to his readers:

Discourse is not life: its time is not your time; in it, you will not be reconciled to death; you may have killed God beneath the weight of all that you have said; but don't imagine that, with all that you are saying, you will make a man that will live longer than he.

This message, consisting of nothing but a series of negations, is also typical of Foucault's discourse, which always tends towards the oracular and to intimations of apocalypse. *His* imagination is 'always at the end of an era'. But the vision is of what can *not* be expected at the end of time. This supreme anti-teleologist resists the lure of any definitive ending, just as he delights in beginnings that open in 'free play', discoveries of paradoxes, and intimations of the folly underlying any 'will to know'.

If, however, Foucault's discourses begin in paradox and end in negative apocalypse, their middles are heavy with what he calls 'positivity', wide (if seemingly capricious) erudition, solemn disclosures of the 'way things really were', aggressive redrawings of the map of cultural history, confident restructurings of the chronicle of 'knowledge'. And even the most sympathetic reader can legitimately ask: How do these middles relate to the beginnings and endings of Foucault's discourse? Their status is difficult to specify in conventional critical terms. For although these middles do *mediate* between the paradoxes which open and the oracular utterances which typically close Foucault's discourses, they have neither the weight of the middle term of a syllogistic argument nor the plausibility of the peripeteia, or sudden reversal, in a narrative.

In fact, Foucault rejects the authority of both logic and conventional narrative. His discourses often suggest a story, but they are never about the same characters, and the events that comprise them are not linked by laws that would permit us to understand some as causes and others as effects. Foucault's 'histories' are as fraught with discontinuities, ruptures, gaps, and lacunae as his arguments. If he continues to fascinate (some of) us, then, it is not because he offers a coherent explanation or even interpretation of our current cultural incoherence, but rather because he denies the authority which the distinction coherence/incoherence has enjoyed in Western thought since Plato. He seeks, not the 'ground', but rather the 'space' within which this distinction arose.

Because he seeks a space rather than a ground, Foucault's discourse unfolds seemingly without restraint, apparently without end. There are now nine books, many essays and interviews, prefaces to reprints of older works, manifestos, and so forth—a flood of what he calls 'utterances' (*énoncés*) which threatens to swamp even the most admiring reader. He has recently (1976) published the first volume of a projected six-volume *History of Sexuality*. What are we to make of this interminable 'series' of texts? How are we to receive it? What are we to do with it?

If we were to follow what Foucault claims to be his own critical principles, we should not be able to refer the whole body of texts, the *œuvre*, to any presiding authorial intention, to any originating event in the life of the author, or to the historical context in which the discourse arises. We should not even be able to speak about its 'impact' or 'influence' on a specific group of readers or to situate Foucault himself within a 'tradition' of discourse. We could not ask, as his most hostile critics have done, whether his statements of fact are true or false, whether his interpretations are valid, or whether his reconstructions of the historical record are plausible. And this because Foucault denies the concreteness of the referent and rejects the notion that there is a 'reality' which precedes discourse and reveals its face to a prediscursive 'perception'. We cannot, as he reminds us in the passages quoted above, ask, On what authority do you speak?, because Foucault sets the free play of his own discourse over against *all* authority. He aspires to a discourse that is free in a radical sense, a discourse that dissolves its own authority, a discourse that opens upon a 'silence' in which only 'things' exist in their irreducible Difference, resisting every impulse to find a Sameness uniting them all in any order whatsoever.

There is, however, one conventional critical concept which appears to escape Foucault's ire. This is the concept of style. He does not explicitly make much of this concept; but he invokes it often enough without qualification to permit its use in the effort to characterize, at least in a preliminary way, the nature of his own discourse. Also, when we have eliminated all of the possible 'authorities' that we might ordinarily appeal to in order to delineate the ground of his discourse, we are still left with the constancies which give to his various texts a unitary tone, mode of address, manner of speaking, attack on the process of *énonciation*; what, in his essay on the novelist Alain Robbe-Grillet, he calls its 'aspect' and what in other places he calls simply 'style'.

In an aside in *The Archaeology of Knowledge*, Foucault defines style as 'a certain constant manner of utterance'. This definition is revealing of what we should look for in our attempts to characterize Foucault's own, obviously highly self-conscious, style. On his own terms, however, we should not fall victim to any banal distinction between style and content, or distinguish between 'what is said' and 'how it is said', because the saying, the 'utterance' (*énonciation*), is what *constitutes* a 'content', a 'referent', or an 'object' of discourse. Until discourse arises against the silence of mere existence or within the 'murmur' of a pre-verbal 'agitation of things', there is no distinction between signifier and signified, subject and object, sign and meaning. Or rather, these distinctions are products of the discursive 'event'. But this event remains oblivious to its real purpose, which is merely to be and to mask the arbitrariness of its existence as simple utterance. And the manner of this simultaneous disclosure and concealment in discourse is its *style*.

Discourse need not have come into existence at all, Foucault tells us. That it did come into existence at a certain time in the order of things suggests its contingency—and points to a time when, like that 'humanity' which is a hypostatization of the fictive subject of discourse, it will come to an end. Meanwhile, discourse eludes all determination, logical, grammatical, or rhetorical, precisely in so far as such determinations are themselves products of discourse's capacity to hide its origin in a play of signifiers which are their own signifieds. It is the mode of this play that constitutes the essence of style. When it displays a 'certain constant manner' of elaboration, we are in the presence of a discourse *with* style. And the highest style, it would seem, is that which self-consciously makes of this play its own object of representation.

So much is shown by Foucault himself in the only one of his works that can legitimately be classified as a 'stylistic analysis' in the conventional sense of the term, his study of the proto-surrealist writer, Raymond Roussel. Here, after a discussion of the traditional rhetorical theory of tropes as set forth by the eighteenth-century grammarian Dumarsais, he remarks: 'Style is the possibility, at once hidden and indicated, under the sovereign necessity of the words used, of saying the same thing, but differently.' Foucault then goes on to characterize Roussel's language, in terms that might well be applied to his own discourse, as 'reversed style' which 'seeks surreptitiously to say two things with the same words'. Roussel makes of the 'twist [*torsion*], that easy turn of words which ordinarily permits them to "lie" [*bouger*] by virtue of a tropological movement and which gives to them their profound freedom, . . . a pitiless circle which leads words back to their point of departure by the force of a compelling law'. The 'bending [*flexion*] of the style becomes its circular negation'.

This notion of a reversed style is apt for characterizing Foucault's own discourse, because like Roussel he does not wish 'to duplicate [*doubler*] the reality [*réel*] of another world, but by means of the spontaneous redoublings of language, to *discover* an unsuspected space and to *recover* therein things never yet said'. Foucault's discourse arises in that 'tropological space' which, like Roussel, he considers as 'a colourless domain in language and which reveals in the very interior of the word its own insidious void, barren and confined'. Finally, also like Roussel, Foucault considers this void as 'a lacuna to be extended as far as possible and to be measured meticulously'. This 'absence' at the heart of language, Foucault takes to be evidence of 'an absolute vacancy of being, which it is necessary to invest, master, and fill up [*combler*] by pure invention'.

The idea of style used to characterize Roussel's discourse

appears increasingly in Foucault's own works as a way of characterizing discourse in general. A 'certain constant manner of utterance', arising in the tropological space which at once reflects and refuses the 'vacancy of being', finding its own rule of dispersion in the capacity of words to say the same thing in different ways or say different things with the same words, circling back upon itself to take its own modality of articulation as its signified, coming to an end as arbitrarily as it began, but leaving a verbal something in the place of the nothing which occasioned it—all this can stand for discourse as well as style in Foucault's thought. To conceive discourse in this way, Foucault tells us in his inaugural lecture in the Collège de France in 1971 (translated as 'The Discourse on Language'), would be to free it from subjection to the myth of 'signification'.

Nine years earlier, in *The Birth of the Clinic* (1963), he had asked: 'But must the things said, elsewhere and by others, be treated exclusively in accordance with the play of signifier and signified, as a series of themes present more or less implicitly to one another?' And he had concluded that, if the 'facts of discourse' were 'treated not as autonomous nuclei of multiple significations, but as events and functional segments gradually coming together to form a system', then 'the meaning of an utterance [*énoncé*] would be defined not by the treasure of intentions that it might contain, revealing and concealing it at the same time, but by the difference that articulates it upon the real or possible statements, which are contemporary with it or to which it is opposed in the linear series of time'.

The crucial terms in this passage, which points to the possibility of 'a systematic history of discourses', are 'events', 'functional segments', 'system', and the notion of the play of 'difference' within the system thus constituted. The 'regulatory principles of analysis' of discourse, Foucault then makes clear in 'The Discourse on Language', are the notions of 'event, series, regularity, and the possible conditions of existence'. 'Style' is the name we will give to the mode of existence of word-events arranged in a series displaying regularity and having specifiable conditions of existence. These conditions of existence are not to be sought in some correlation of 'what is said' with an 'order of things' which pre-exists and sanctions one 'order of words' as against another. They are to be found in two kinds of restraint placed on discourse since the time of its domestication by the Greeks: external, on the one side, consisting of the repressions or displacements corresponding to those governing the expression of desire or the exercise of power; and internal, on the other, consisting of certain rules of classification, ordering, and distribution, and certain 'rarefactions' which have the effect of masking discourse's true nature as 'free play'.

What is at work in discourse—as in everything else—is always 'desire and power', but in order for the aims of desire and power to be realized, discourse must ignore its basis in them. This is why (as Foucault goes on to say in 'The Discourse on Language') discourse, at least since the rout of the Sophists by Plato, unfolds always in the service of the 'will to truth'. Discourse wishes to 'speak the truth', but in order to do this it must mask from itself its service to desire and power, must indeed mask from itself the fact that it is itself a manifestation of the operations of these two forces.

Like desire and power, discourse unfolds 'in every society' within the context of external restraints which appear as 'rules of exclusion', rules which determine what can be said and not said, who has the right to speak on a given subject, what will constitute reasonable and what 'foolish' actions, what will count as 'true' and what as 'false'. These rules limit the conditions of discourse's existence in different ways in different times and places. Whence the distinction, arbitrary but taken for granted in all societies, between 'proper', reasonable, responsible, sane, and truthful discourse, on the one side, and 'improper', unreasonable, irresponsible, insane, and erroneous discourse, on the other. Foucault himself vacillates between the impulse to justify the discourse of madness, criminality, and sickness (whence his celebration of such writers as Sade, Hölderlin, Nietzsche, Artaud, Lautréamont, Roussel, and so on), on the one hand, and his constantly reaffirmed aim to probe beneath the distinction between proper and improper discourse, in order to explicate the ground on which the distinction itself arises, on the other. Despite this vacillation, his probings take the form of 'diagnoses' intended to reveal the 'pathology' of a mechanism of control which governs discursive and non-discursive activity alike.

As for the internal restraints placed on discourse, the 'rarefactions' noted above, all these are functions of the distinction, as false as it is insidious, between an order of words and an order of things, which makes discourse itself possible. What is at work here is some principle of subordination, the vertical equivalent, we might say, of the horizontal principle of exclusion operative in the external restraints. At the base of every principle of subordination operative in discourse is the distinction between the signifier and the signified, or rather the fiction of the adequacy of the former to the latter in every 'proper' discourse. Whence the conventionalist theories of discourse which seek to obscure its status as mere 'event' in order to ground it in a subject (the author), an originating experience (such as writing or reading), or an activity (discourse conceived as mediation between perception and consciousness, or between consciousness and the world, as in philosophical or scientific theories of language).

These conventionalist theories, Foucault argues in 'The Discourse on Language', must be dismissed as mere manifestations of the power of discourse to nullify itself by 'placing itself at the disposal of the signifier'. All of this, reflective of a profound 'logophobia' in Western culture, has the effect of averting the very real 'powers and dangers' of discourse. These derive from the capacity of discourse to reveal, in the free play of words, the arbitrariness of *every* rule and norm, even those on which society itself, with its rules of exclusion and hierarchical order, is founded. In order to free discourse from these restraints and to open it up once more to the project of saying everything that can be said in as many ways as it can be said—in order, in a word, to preside over the dissolution of discourse by closing the gap opened up by the distinction between 'words and things'—Foucault undertakes to expose the dark underside of every discursive formation purporting to serve 'the will of truth'.

This was the more or less clearly stated purpose of his earlier books, *Madness and Civilization* (1961), *Birth of the Clinic* (1963), and *The Order of Things* (1966). These dealt with the discourses of psychiatry, medicine, and the human sciences respectively, and the ways in which official discourse perceived, classified, and distributed such insubstantial 'things' as 'sanity', 'health', and 'knowledge' at different times in the history of Western culture. These books sought to demonstrate that the distinctions between madness and sanity, sickness and health, and truth and error were always a function of the modality of discourse prevailing in centres of social power at different periods. In Foucault's view, this modality was in turn less a *product* of an autonomous exchange between hypothesis and observation, or theory and practice, than the *basis* of whatever theory and practice prevailed in a given period. And it followed for him that, finally, the modern history of Western man's 'will to knowledge' had been less a progressive development towards 'enlightenment' than a product of an endless interaction between desire and power within the system of exclusions which made different kinds of society possible.

This structure of deception and duplicity underlying all discourse was more systematically explicated in *The Archaeology of Knowledge* and 'The Discourse on Language'; and it has been further illuminated and specified in the two books which have appeared after these two essays: *Discipline and Punish. The Birth of the Prison* (1975); and *The History of Sexuality* (1976).

These two recent works are manifestly studies of the relationship between the desire for power and the power of desire as revealed in the controls exercised by society over two social types which have threatened its authority throughout time: the criminal on the one side, and the sexual deviant on the other. In the practices of incarceration and exclusion respectively, the power of discourse is confirmed by its *creation* of the human types with which these practices are intended to deal. As thus envisaged, both works are studies of the 'discourse of power' in conflict with the 'discourse of desire'.

Wherever Foucault looks, he finds nothing but discourse; and wherever discourse arises, he finds a struggle between those groups which claim the 'right' to discourse and those which are denied the right to their own discourse. In *Discipline and Punish* and *The History of Sexuality*, he comes out more fully on the side of the victims of this discourse of power and against the 'authority' of those who exercise the power of 'exclusion' under the guise of a simple service to 'truth'. But the authority of his own discourse remains unspecified. What, we may still ask, is its modality, its 'right', and its relationship to the order of discourse of the time and place in which *it* arises?

Thus far, I have touched only the surface of Foucault's own

discourse and suggested that its claim to authority must, on his own terms, derive from the 'certain constant manner of utterance', that is to say, the style which characterizes it. This style, again on his own terms, cannot be identified as that of a discipline; because Foucault refuses the conventional titles of philosopher, historian, sociologist of knowledge, and so forth. It cannot be identified with those looser groupings which, in 'The Discourse on Language', he calls 'fellowships of discourse', since in his major works he resolutely ignores the work of most of his contemporaries. And most certainly it cannot be linked to any doctrinal orthodoxy of a religious or sectarian sort.

If Foucault were writing this essay, he might situate his discourse, and classify its style, by reference to what he himself calls the *'épistème'* of our age, that is to say, 'the total set of relations that unite, at a given period, the discursive practices that give rise to epistemological figures, sciences, and possibly formalized systems' of knowledge (cf. *The Archaeology of Knowledge*). But once more, in Foucault's own terms, the *épistème* of an age cannot be known by those who work under its aegis. In any event, according to him, we are at the end of one epistemic configuration and at the beginning of another. We exist in the gap between two *épistèmes*, one dying, the other not yet born—of which, however, the 'mad' poets and artists of the last century and a half were the heralds.

The virtually unquestioned authority which Foucault grants to these heralds suggests the tradition of discourse to which he would wish to belong—if 'tradition' were an honorific term to him, and if it could be used to classify a group of artists as different as Hölderlin, Goya, Nietzsche, Van Gogh, Rilke, Artaud, and, above all, Sade. Foucault values the brilliant opacity, the dark superficiality, the casual profundity of those writers who inhabit the silent places left by the discourse of 'normal' men. His debt to them would permit us to place him among the anarchists—if he shared their utopian optimism; or among the nihilists—if he possessed any standard by which to justify his preference for 'nothing' over 'something'. But Foucault has none of the *directness* of his heroes. He cannot *say* anything directly. And this because he has no confidence in the power of words to represent either 'things' or 'thoughts'.

It is not surprising, then, that Foucault's own discourse tends to assume the form of what the critic Northrop Frye calls the 'existential projection' of a rhetorical trope into a metaphysics. This rhetorical trope is catachresis, and Foucault's style not only displays a profusion of the various figures sanctioned by catachresis, such as paradox, oxymoron, chiasmus, hysteron proteron, metalepsis, prolepsis, antonomasia, paronomasia, antiphrasis, hyperbole, litotes, irony, and so on; his own discourse stands as an abuse of everything for which 'normal' or 'proper' discourse stands. It *looks* like history, like philosophy, like criticism, but it stands over against these discourses as ironic antithesis. It even assumes a position superior to that of Foucault's own heroes, for Foucault's 'discourse about discourses' seeks to effect the dissolution of Discourse itself. This is why I call it catachretic.

In traditional rhetorical theory, the notion of catachresis (Latin: *abusio*; English: 'misuse') presupposes the distinction between the literal and the figurative meanings of words, or more generally, the validity of the distinction between 'proper' and 'improper' usage. Since for Foucault all words have their origin in a 'tropological space' in which the sign enjoys a 'freedom . . . to alight' upon any aspect of the entity it is meant to signify, then the distinction between literal and figurative meanings goes by the board—except as an indication of the power of discourse to constitute 'literality' through the application of a consistent rule of signification. This means that *all* verbal constructions are basically catachretic, inasmuch as no union of any signifier with any signified is 'natural' or given by 'necessity'. Literal meaning, like 'proper' usage, is the product of the application of a norm, social in nature, hence arbitrary, rather than a result of the operation of a law (see *The Order of Things*).

But Foucault seems to agree with the eighteenth-century rhetoricians and with Pierre Fontanier, the nineteenth-century French systematizer of their theories, that the kinds of relationships which the sign may have with the entity it is intended to represent are limited to four: depending on whether the sign 'alights' on 'some internal element' of the entity to be represented by it, some point 'adjacent' to the entity, some figure 'similar' to the entity, or some figure manifestly 'dissimilar' to it. This classification yields what Foucault himself, in *The Order of Things*, calls the 'fundamental figures so well known to rhetoric: synecdoche, metonymy, and catachresis (or metaphor, if the analogy is less immediately perceptible)'. Each represents a different modality of construing the relationship between signs and the things they are meant to signify.

Catachresis enjoys a privileged place in Foucault's own conception of tropes, because, for him, no two things are similar to one another in their particularity. *All* language therefore constitutes an abuse in so far as it gives a single name to things different in their 'internal natures', their location in space, or their external attributes. It is *all* catachretic in origin, although the myth of literal or 'proper' meaning obscures this origin and thereby permits the reduction of catachresis to the status of a figure of rhetoric which arises out of a simple misuse of 'proper' speech. It follows that, if discourse takes its origin in a tropological space, it must unfold within one or another of the fundamental modalities of figuration in which a relationship between 'words and things' can be construed. Consequently, the style of a discourse, its 'certain constant manner of utterance', can be characterized in terms of the dominant trope which establishes the originating relationship between 'words and things' and determines 'what can be said' about things in 'proper' discourse.

Foucault goes even further: the dominant trope of a given community of discourse determines both 'what can be seen' in the world and 'what can be known' about it. Tropology thus constitutes the basis of what Foucault calls the *'épistème'* of an age in the history of thought and expression. It also provides him with a way of characterizing the sequence of *épistèmes* that makes up the 'history' of thought about the topics he has analysed in his major books: madness, clinical medicine, the human sciences, incarceration, and sexuality. This theory of tropes is what underlies and therefore clarifies his own characterization of his 'archaeological' method: 'What archaeology wishes to uncover is primarily the play of analogies and differences . . .' (*The Archaeology of Knowledge*).

'Analogies and differences . . .' In the beginning, Foucault's enabling myth tells us, everything was simply what it was. 'Sameness' or analogy arose with speech, the gathering of different things under a single name. This gave birth to the concepts of the type, the proposition, and knowledge conceived as the classification of the Different in terms of Sameness, Similitude, or Resemblance.

'All error', says Kant in his *Logic*, echoing Bacon and anticipating Darwin, 'has its origin in resemblance.' Foucault expands this dictum. For him, resemblance is also the source of everything that passes for 'truth' or 'knowledge'. The perception of the Same in the Different, or of Sameness in the *interplay* of Similarities and Differences as it appears in any aggregate of entities, lies at the base of myth, religion, science, and philosophy alike. But not only this; the perception of Sameness is the basis of social praxis too, of that manipulation of Sameness and Difference which, first, permits the social group to identify itself as a unity, and then to disperse itself into a hierarchy of more or less different groupings, some 'more alike' than others, some more sane, more healthy, more rational, more normal, more *human*, than others.

The perception of 'the Same in the Different' and of 'the Different in the Same' is the origin of all hierarchy in social practice, as it is the origin of syntax in grammar and of logic in thought. Hierarchy itself derives from that Fall of man into language, and the capacity of speech to 'say two things with the same words' or 'the same thing with different words'. Discourse arises when this capacity of speech becomes highly developed, formalized, submitted to rules, and unfolds under the aegis of a normative concept such as 'the permitted versus the prohibited', 'the rational versus the irrational', or 'the true versus the false'. But the limit on what can be said, and *a fortiori* what can be seen and thought, is set by the 'error' which resides at the heart of any verbal representation of the 'real'.

This limit is reached when Difference asserts its rights against Sameness. Then discourse, motivated by the 'will to truth' which informs it, shifts to another mode of construing the relation between 'words and things'. Typically, in Foucault's schema, every 'discursive' formation undergoes a finite number of such shifts before reaching the limits of the *épistème* that sanctions its operations. This number corresponds to the fundamental modes of figuration identified by the theory of tropology: metaphor, metonymy, synecdoche, and irony (which is here understood as *self-conscious* catachresis).

Thus, for example, in *Madness and Civilization*, the 'discourse on madness' which unfolds in the West between the late Middle Ages and our own time is shown to go through four phases. First, in the sixteenth century, madness is removed from its status as a sign of sanctity, repository of a divine truth, and simultaneously differentiated from and identified with a specifically human wisdom, as in the character of the Wise Fool and the traditional subject of the 'praise of folly'. Then, in the seventeenth and eighteenth centuries, what Foucault calls the 'Classical age', madness is set over against reason in the mode of contiguity or adjacency, in the way that, in the formal thought of the age, humanity was set over against bestiality or reason against unreason. This mode of conceiving the relation between madness and sanity is reflected in (and finds its confirmation in) the treatment of those designated as insane, who are not only expelled from society by virtue of their 'differentness', but are also confined in special places at the limits of society, 'hospitals', where they are imprisoned and 'treated' along with those other 'dangerous' deviants from the social norm, criminals and paupers.

Then, in the nineteenth century, the relationship between madness and sanity changes again, reflected in the reforms of Pinel and Tuke, who 'liberated' the insane from association with criminals and paupers, defined them as simply 'sick' rather than essentially different from their 'healthier' counterparts, and identified their illness with a phase in the development of the human organism, as either an arrested form of, or regression to, childhood. The insane were thus at once re-identified with 'normal' humanity, by being identified with one of the latter's phases of development, hence defined as being essentially the same as the latter, and at the same time differentiated from it as requiring a special kind of treatment, usually punitive but always physical, cultivated in the special 'asylums' set up for the insane.

Finally, in the twentieth century, a new way of construing the relation between madness and sanity crystallizes, represented above all by Freud and psychoanalysis, in the theory of which the distinction between sanity and insanity is once more weakened, and the similarities between the two are stressed; and the notion of the 'neurosis' is elaborated as an intermediary term between the two extremes. Foucault honours Freud as the first modern man to 'listen' to what the insane were saying, to try to find the reason in their unreason, the method in their madness. On the other hand, while Freud delivered the patient from 'the existence of the asylum', he did not liberate him from the authority of the doctor himself, that combination of scientist and thaumaturge. In the 'psychoanalytical situation', Foucault maintains in *Madness and Civilization*, 'alienation becomes disalienating because, in the doctor, it becomes a subject.'

The failure to abolish this authoritarian structure, he concludes, both sets the limit on what psychoanalysis can achieve and reveals the 'irony' of its claims to liberate. And this because, although psychoanalysis can 'unravel some of the forms of madness, it remains a stranger to the sovereign enterprise of unreason'. The extent of its alienation from this 'enterprise' is to be measured by its failure to comprehend the heralds of radical freedom, those seers whom sane society nullifies under the name of the 'mad artist'.

Since the end of the eighteenth century, the life of unreason no longer manifests itself except in the lightning-flash of words such as those of Hölderlin, of Nerval, of Nietzsche, or of Artaud—for ever irreducible to those alienations that can be cured, resisting by their own strength that gigantic moral imprisonment which we are in the habit of calling, doubtless by antiphrasis, the liberation of the insane by Pinel and Tuke.

(*Madness and Civilization*)

Foucault's own catachretic reflection on the condition of sanity in the modern world takes its authority from those 'lightning-flashes' which, in the works of art where they appear, 'open a void, a moment of silence, a question without an answer, [and] provoke a breach without reconciliation where the world is forced to question itself'. His celebration of madness is 'beyond irony', since it gives credit to the existence of a 'silence' before the 'differentiation' of madness and sanity occurred.

Arising in that tropological space in which words can 'alight' freely on whatever aspect of the thing they are intended to signify, the history of the 'discourse on madness' displays the possible modalities of this 'alightment'. The modes and tropes which underlie them are, successively, resemblance (metaphor), adjacency (metonymy), essentiality (synecdoche), and what might be called doubling (irony). In its modern phase the discourse on madness takes the form of duplicity, of a doubling-effect, in which madness is identified with both normality *and* genius, is at once brought back into the world in the form of the patient *and* further alienated from it in the form of the mad poet; at once defined as sickness and deviation from the norm *and* tacitly recognized as a standard against which the norm can be measured. Foucault takes his stand in the breach, the gap, the void which opens up between these two faces of madness. And asks, by what authority do *we* presume to 'speak' of either?

The question of authority, the assumption of the power to force conformity to social norms, has increasingly moved to the centre of Foucault's own discourse in the books which followed *Madness and Civilization*, from his study of the 'discourse on sickness' (*The Birth of the Clinic*) to his studies of the 'discourse on criminality' (*Discipline and Punish*) and the 'discourse on sexuality' (*History of Sexuality*). And it is this question which is at the heart of his most influential work, his study of the 'discourse on humanity' (*The Order of Things*).

The Order of Things is about the use and abuse of the 'authority' of the 'human sciences'. In it Foucault wishes to show that the disciplines which deal with man as a social and cultural being are as little 'scientific' as those conceptions of the 'body' which have successively informed medical practice from the sixteenth century to our own day. *The Order of Things* is denser than Foucault's other 'historical' books, because in it he deals with discourses that are more theoretical than practical, or at least ones that do not have the immediate applicability that such discourses as 'psychiatry, medicine, and penology' do. Consequently, he is compelled to consider the *epistemological* authority of the theoretical disciplines which comprise the 'human sciences'. This authority he invests in the *épistème* of an age or a community of discourses, the deep but unacknowledged mode of relating 'words and things' which gives to these discourses their coherence, within and between themselves.

As in the book on madness, so too in *The Order of Things*, Foucault identifies four distinct periods of epistemic coherence: the sixteenth century, the *âge classique*, the nineteenth century, and our own age. Each period is studied 'vertically', that is to say, archaeologically, rather than 'horizontally' or historically. The strategy is to work from texts or fragments of texts produced during a given period, without any concern for the biographies of the authors who wrote them, solely with the aim of identifying a distinctive 'discursive mode' shared by all the important texts of an age or epoch.

What counts as an 'important' text, of course, is one which displays evidence of the appearance of a discursive mode different from that which prevailed in the preceding age. Foucault is less concerned with the 'classic' text, the text which is fully systematized and realized in accordance with the *épistème* which sanctions its discourse, than with the text which marks out a new domain of enquiry, or rather constitutes new 'positivities' and 'empiricities' on the basis of a new conceptualization of consciousness's relation to the world. Thus, for example, in his analyses of the sciences of biology, economics, and philology in the nineteenth century, he is less interested in (indeed, all but ignores) Darwin, Marx, and Wilamowitz, than in Cuvier, Ricardo, and Bopp. The latter trio are regarded as the true 'inventors' of the new domains of enquiry: biology, economics, and philology, respectively.

Before the appearance of these three thinkers, Foucault argues, the sciences of biology, economics, and philology did not exist. No more than 'man' existed as an object of study prior to the late eighteenth century. Before this time, 'natural history', 'wealth', and 'general grammar' were the principal domains of the field of 'human sciences', just as before the late eighteenth century, the concept of 'man' was obscured by the more general concept of 'creation' or the 'order of things' of which the 'human thing' was but one, and by no means a privileged, instance.

It is folly, then, Foucault argues, to imagine, as conventional historians of ideas are inclined to do, that there are discrete disciplines developing over long periods of time which have the same objects of enquiry, with only the names by which these objects are called changing and the laws governing them becoming progressively clearer as 'error' is eliminated and 'fact' replaces 'superstition' or mere 'speculation'. For what shall count as error and what as truth, what as fact and what as fancy: these change as arbitrarily as the modes of discourse and the originating *épistèmes* undergo 'mutation'.

One can, of course, speak of the 'influence' of one thinker on another, of precursors and incarnators of intellectual traditions, and even of 'genealogies' of ideas, if one wishes; but one should do so in the full realization that such concepts are legitimate only within the epistemic presuppositions of nineteenth-century discourse, a discourse which is not even that of our intellectual fathers but, at best, of our grandfathers. For new 'master disciplines' in the human sciences were constituted on the eve of our own era, in ethnology, psychoanalysis, and linguistics, all of which orient their 'true' practitioners, not along the horizontal axis of 'befores and afters', as nineteenth-century historicist disciplines did, but along the vertical axis of 'surfaces and depths'—and continually point to the insoluble mystery which the notion of a depth without a bottom calls forth.

Knowledge in the human sciences thus no longer takes the form in our age of the search for Similarities and Resemblances (as it did in the sixteenth century), Contiguities and Tables of Relationships (as it did in the Classical age), or Analogies and Successions (as it did in the nineteenth century), but rather Surfaces and Depths—generated by the return to consciousness of the nameless 'silence' which underlies and makes possible the forms of all discourse, even that of 'science' itself. This is why, in our age, knowledge tends to take the form either of Formalizations or Interpretations, and unfolds within an awareness of consciousness's incapacity ever to locate its own origin and of language's inability to reveal a subject; and this because of the inevitable interposition of discourse between the Subject and its putative 'subject-matter'. This is why 'The whole curiosity of our thought now resides in the question: What is language, and how can we find a way round it in order to make it appear in itself, in all its plenitude?' (*The Order of Things*).

But this curiosity can never be satisfied, Foucault maintains, because: 'The object of the human sciences is not language (though it is spoken by men alone); it is that being [man] which, from the interior of language by which he is surrounded, represents to himself, by speaking, the sense of the words or propositions he utters, and finally provides himself with a representation of language itself.' Not even the modern science of linguistics can specify 'what language must be in order to structure . . . what is . . . not in itself either word or discourse, and in order to articulate itself on the pure forms of knowledge'. Indeed, it is not in science at all but in literature, and a literature 'dedicated to language', that 'we are led back to the place that Nietzsche and Mallarmé signposted when the first asked: Who speaks?, and the second saw his glittering answer in the Word itself'.

A literature so dedicated 'gives prominence, in all their empirical vivacity, to the fundamental forms of finitude', the most fundamental form of which is death. This literature, which presses beyond madness to 'that formless, mute, unsignifying region where language can find its freedom', signals the 'disappearance of Discourse' and with it, the 'disappearance of man'. For:

Man had been a figure occurring between two modes of language; or, rather, he was constituted only when language, having been situated within representation and, as it were, dissolved in it, freed itself from that situation only at the cost of its own fragmentation: man composed his own figure in the interstices of that fragmented language.

(ibid.)

That 'man', of which humanists speak so eloquently and confidently, is thus considered to have no specific being in the world, no essence, no objectivity. The history of the human sciences shows us efforts to locate the nature of man in his being as 'living, producing, and speaking' animal; but this 'living, producing, speaking' themselves dissolve and escape identification, behind the discourses intended to reveal their substance—only to reappear, in a new guise, as the subject of new 'sciences', when a given notion of 'life, labour, or language' finds its limit in language itself.

The crucial change, or rather 'mutation', in the history of Western thought, *The Order of Things* contends, is that which 'situated language within representation', charged words with the task of serving as transparent and unambiguous signs of the 'things' that made up 'reality'. This elevation of words to a special status among things created a gap within which 'Classical' discourse, the discourse of the Enlightenment, could unfold. Hidden behind its status as simple 'representation' of the real, this discourse was able to offer *its own form* as the obscure content of reality. And because discourse was thus privileged, reality inevitably took on the aspects of the linguistic mode in which it was presented to consciousness. Since, in the eighteenth century, language was regarded as timeless, as having no history, and universal, as being governed everywhere by the same grammatical and syntactical rules, then not only knowledge but also its object, man, were considered to be characterized by this same timelessness and universality of determination. Accordingly, knowledge aspired to the construction of 'tables', in which the vocabulary, grammar, and syntax of 'reality' would be revealed, its simple elements named, its species and genera unambiguously determined, and its combinatory rules made manifest.

This dream of a *mathesis universalis* has remained the legacy of the sciences, both physical and social, ever since. Its inadequacy to reality became evident, however, at the furthest limit of its development in the nineteenth century, when names were seen to be variable in what they could designate, when the taxonomies revealed their incapacity to accommodate certain 'borderline' cases or 'monsters', and when the combinatory rules failed of all precise prediction. In the early nineteenth century, it dawned on Western man that not only he, but language also, had a 'history'. But Foucault does not see this intensification of 'historical consciousness' as an advance in learning, a progressive movement in the history of thought caused by realization of the 'error' contained in the earlier conception of knowledge. On the contrary, the new historical sense was a function of a profound 'time-anxiety', a realization that the Classical age had no place for time in its *épistème*; or rather, had purchased its certitude at the expense of any awareness of the reality of time, of the *finitude* of existence.

Whence the radical reconstitution of the whole domain of knowledge in the nineteenth century, its reconceptualization in terms, not of Contiguity and the (spatialized) Table, but of Analogy and (temporal) Succession—evidence of a hope that 'things' were at least affiliated in time if not related in space. Whence, too, therefore, the proliferation of those great philosophies of history (of Hegel, Marx, and so many others), and even more of those concrete 'historical narratives' (of Ranke, Mommsen, Michelet, and so on), in which the age abounded. 'Life, labour, and language' were also historicized in the nineteenth century, in the hope that by the study of their evolution in time, their deeper unities would be discovered. But this enterprise, carried out most completely in biology, economics, and philology, was as much doomed to failure as that of the Classical age. For the 'origin' which it relentlessly pursued just as relentlessly receded from any positive identification. The historical approach to the study of 'life, labour, and language' revealed neither the Origin nor the Subject of these activities; all it revealed, wherever 'knowledge' looked, was infinite Difference and endless Change.

This apprehension of the play of Difference and Change, Foucault maintains, motivates the leading 'human sciences' of our century: ethnology, psychoanalysis, and linguistics. Each of these disciplines gives a place of privilege to language, and hence approaches closer to the void in which discourse arises than its earlier counterpart. However, in their propensity to divide their objects (culture, consciousness, and language) into a 'surface' and a 'depth', and in their faith in their capacity to discover a Subject lurking in those depths, they too reveal their bondage to the myth of Sameness. This is why Foucault, in the Preface to *The Order of Things*, characterizes his book as 'a history of resemblance, . . . a history of the Same'; and why, at the end of this book, he writes: 'It is apparent how modern reflection . . . moves towards a certain thought of the Same—in which Difference is the same thing as identity.' Over against the Same-Different distinction (or rather, meta-distinction, for this dyad is what justifies 'distinction' itself), he sets the notion of the Other, whose history provides the ironic antithesis to that of the Same. This Other's history is inscribed within the 'discourses' on madness, sickness, criminality, and sexuality, on the basis of which it has always been 'shut away'.

Foucault's work since *The Order of Things* can thus be understood as a specification and amplification of the insight with which that book ended:

Man has not been able to describe himself as a configuration in the *épistème* without thought at the same time discovering, both in itself and outside itself, at its borders yet also in its very warp and woof, an element of darkness, an apparently inert density in which it is embedded, an unthought which it contains entirely, yet in which it is also caught. The unthought (whatever name we give it) is not lodged in man like a shrivelled-up nature or a stratified history; it is, in relation to man, the Other: the Other that is not only a brother but a twin, not of man, nor in man, but beside him and at the same time, in an identical newness, in an unavoidable duality.

The Order of Things is a 'history of the Same—of that which, for a given culture, is both dispersed and related, therefore to be distinguished by kinds and to be collected together into identities'. *Discipline and Punish* and *The History of Sexuality*, like *Madness and Civilization* and *The Birth of the Clinic*, are histories of 'the Other', that which is 'shut away' and hidden 'in order to reduce its otherness', that which is regarded, always pre-judicially, as the abnormal.

In 1973, Foucault published the results of a collective investigation, made by his students in a seminar, of a famous murder which occurred in the early nineteenth century, *'Moi, Pierre Rivière, ayant égorgé ma mère, ma soeur et mon frère . . .'.* This was a case-study of the ways in which different kinds of discourse, medico-psychiatric, journalistic, and political, revealed the workings of 'power' in their 'analyses' and recommended 'treatment' of the murderer. Foucault's own interest in this case stemmed, obviously, from the insight it provided into the function of 'murder' in marking the limits between legality, on the one hand, and illegality on the other. After all, he reminds us, society distinguishes among different kinds of killing: criminal, martial, political (the assassination), and accidental. In the bourgeois society taking shape in the early nineteenth century, however, 'murder' had an especial fascination; and accounts of murders, such as Pierre Rivière's famous *mémoire* of his crime, an especial popularity.

The 'universal success' of these *récits* manifests 'the desire to know and to tell how men have been able to rebel against [*se lever contre*] power, break the law, to expose themselves to death by means of death'. What these *récits* and their popularity reveal, Foucault concludes, is a 'battle which was taking shape, on the eve of revolutionary struggles and imperialist wars, over two rights, less different than they appear at first sight: the right to kill and have killed; [and] the right to speak and to recount'. Apparently, popular and official opinion alike were more outraged by Rivière's presumption in writing about his crime than they were by his committing it. His discourse seemed to have 'doubled' the crime, making him the 'author' of it twice over; first 'in fact', secondly in 'history'. Rivière, in fact, did not try to excuse himself from the crime, but rather to situate it in the 'discourse of murder' which, in its official form, both sanctioned and prohibited 'killing'. In daring to give his own account of the crime, he set his own discourse over against every official one: legal, medical, political, and folkloric.

The fact that his act involved a parricide brought it close to the fundamental concerns of society: the similarity of parricide to regicide, or indeed, to any kind of political assassination, had long been recognized, in folklore and law alike. The nature of the crime, therefore, had both social and political implications, since it raised the question of the authority of the parent over the child in the family, in the first instance, and that of the state over the citizen, in the second. In setting his own 'discourse' over against all official discourses, Rivière effectively claimed his own freedom to act however he wished, in conformity to his own desires; and by implication he challenged the authority of society, whether vested in the family, the state, the law, science, or popular opinion, to judge him in *its* terms.

By remanding the sentence of death and consigning Rivière to life imprisonment, the State in the person of the king reasserted its authority while simultaneously masking it behind an act of grace. In deciding that Rivière had been insane and not, therefore, the '*auteur*' of his crime, it also nullified his claims to be the *auteur* of his own discourse about it. Instead of being *auteur*, he was defined simply as '*autre*' and put away in the prison which, in the modern, totalitarian state, is the potential destiny of any deviant from the norms of society. That all deviancy is implicitly considered to be criminal, insane, or sick, Foucault had sought to show in his studies of the discourses of penology, psychiatry, and medicine. That the notion of deviancy as crime, madness, and sickness arises within the economy of discourse itself, in the distinction between proper and improper discourse, is also the explicit message of '*Moi, Pierre Rivière, ayant égorgé ma mère, ma soeur et mon frère . . .*'.

This contention is further documented in *Discipline and Punish* and *The History of Sexuality*. The historical framework of the arguments presented in these two books is the same as that found in earlier works: the transition from the *épisteme* of the Classical age to that of the nineteenth century (or rather the mutation of the latter out of the former) is the centre of interest. The celebration of the relative openness of sixteenth-century society *vis-à-vis* criminality, on the one hand, and sexuality on the other, is found in these works also; as is the suggestion that our own time is undergoing another change of momentous impact. And as in *The Birth of the Clinic* especially, here too changes in medical and psychiatric discourse are linked to the impulse towards totalitarian control which Foucault conceives to be intrinsic to modern society. But in *The History of Sexuality* especially, this totalitarian impulse is represented as being more powerful, more fraught with consequences, more apocalyptic than it appears in his earlier works. And this because the 'discourse on sexuality' in our time unfolds in the effort to gain total control over the whole individual—over the body, to be sure, but over the psyche also.

Discipline and Punish prepares us for this analysis of totalitarianism by explicating the function of the prison in modern society. Product of the modern 'discourse on criminality', the prison serves as a model of the '*société disciplinaire*' of which it is the first institutional manifestation. Invented in the nineteenth century, different from the dungeons and châteaux of incarceration which littered the landscape of the Classical age, the prison is committed less to the hiding and confinement of criminals than to their 'reformation' into ideal types of what the citizen outside them should be. The prison reforms of the nineteenth century, however, far from being the evidence of growing enlightenment and humanitarianism which they are conventionally presented as being, reflect a new conception of the ideal society, a new conception of deviancy, and new ways of dealing with it.

In the totally ordered, hierocratized space of the nineteenth-century prison, the prisoner is put under constant surveillance, discipline, and education in order to transform him into what power as now organized in society demands that everyone become: docile, productive, hard-working, self-regulating, conscience-ridden, in a word, 'normal' in every way. Similar reforms, seemingly inspired by the new, enlightened conception of the citizen as a 'responsible' human being, were carried out during the same period in schools, military systems, and places of work. Justified by the new social sciences which supposedly promoted a new, and more enlightened, idea of human nature, culture, and society, these disciplinary apparatuses (Foucault's word is the virtually untranslatable '*dispositifs*') secretly conceal within their several 'discourses' the ideal of the prisons organized on their bases. In the sixteenth century, Foucault argues, criminals and heretics were publicly tortured, mutilated, and put to death, in a 'spectacle' intended to remind the 'subject' of the sovereign's right to punish, his right to 'kill'. But at least this treatment was open and direct, exacted on the body of the prisoner rather than on his whole being, and possessed at its worst the not unenviable virtue of 'candour'. By its nature, torture *taught* that authority was based on force, and showed by implication that the subject had a 'right' to take the law into his own hands, and to answer force with force, if he had the power to do so.

Modern legal systems and the penal systems they serve (rather than the reverse) represent a social authority which masks itself behind professions of humanistic concern for the citizen, humanitarian principles of social organization, and altruistic ideals of service and enlightenment. But this authority, as sovereign in practice as any absolute monarch claimed to be in theory, seeks to make society into an extended prison, in which discipline becomes an end in itself; and conformity to a norm which governs every aspect of life, and especially desire, becomes the only principle both of law and morality.

Thus summarized, this sounds very much like the kind of ranting we normally associate with conservative opponents of the power of the centralized state, or a liberal defence of the individual against a 'society' intent on violating his rights. It sounds a little like Camus in *The Rebel*, opposing 'totalitarianism' and holding up the prospect of an amiable anarchy as a desirable alternative. But if, in *Discipline and Punish*, Foucault seems to be defending the individual against society, it is not because he credits any idea of 'natural rights' or the sanctity of a 'contract' between the members of society, or between them and their government. Far from honouring the notions of rights and contract, Foucault abandons the notion of the natural itself.

In fact, he argues that, wherever it appears in the discourses of the human sciences, the natural always conceals within it the aspect of a 'norm', so that any 'law' supposedly derived from a study of the natural can always be shown to be nothing more than a 'rule' by which to define the 'normal' and to justify the 'disciplining' of those who deviate from the norm, by punishment, incarceration, education, or some other form of 'moral engineering'. The

play of the concepts 'normality' and 'deviancy', and their functioning in the social discourse of our own time, are never more clearly
seen than in the modern human sciences' concern with 'perversion' and the 'pervert'. And this concern is never more apparent
than in the modern 'discourse on sexuality'. To show that these
concepts and this concern are simply elements in a never-ending
conflict between power and desire is the aim of his *History of
Sexuality*. To show how this conflict, in turn, is masked behind a
simple 'desire for knowledge' is the aim of the first volume.

The title of this volume, *La Volonté de savoir* (published in English as
The History of Sexuality, 1978), indicates the matrix of the larger
work: the complex relationships which have taken shape in Western society, since the sixteenth century but especially in the
nineteenth and twentieth centuries, between power, desire, and
knowledge. The stated aim of the full work is to analyse the *'mise en
discours'* of sex and to relate this to the 'polymorphous techniques of
power'. We are to be enlightened, we are promised, about the
'productive processes' which engender 'sex, power, and knowledge', to the end of constructing a veritable 'political economy' of
Western man's 'will to know'. The principal subject of analysis will
be, not sex itself, sexual practices, or the folklore of sex, but rather a
'discourse' which substitutes the abstraction 'sexuality' for the
'body and pleasure' as a 'drive' which underlies every aspect of life
and as the 'mystery' which clothes the 'secret' of life itself.

If, however, in succeeding volumes Foucault follows the outline
given in the first, the work will represent a significant departure
from the notions of cultural history which he has promoted up till
now. First of all, he seems no longer interested in defending the
notion of historical discontinuity, rupture, or mutation on which he
has insisted in previous works. He presents the nineteenth-century
discourse on sexuality as importantly new in what it aspires to and
achieves, but he finds its institutional origins in medieval monastic
discipline, the 'confessional' culture of post-Tridentine religion,
and the 'technology of sex' developed in the eighteenth century.
Secondly, more overtly than in previous works, Foucault grounds
the 'discourse on sexuality' in the larger 'discourse of power', so
much so that, in this work, it seems that he finally reaches a bottom
in his efforts to plumb the *'abîme'* out of which discourse in general

arises. He will, he promises us in his methodological remarks, analyse 'a certain knowledge of sex, in terms not of repression or of law, but of power'; and he then proceeds to define power in such a way as to endow it with all the mystery, all the metaphysicality, with which he claims that power endows sex.

'Power', Foucault says, 'is everywhere . . .'. Moreover, it is not a thing that can be acquired; its relations are immanent in all other kinds of relations (economic, political, etc.); it 'comes from below'; and its relations are both 'intentional and non-subjective'. This suggests that we should not expect from him in future an analysis of the general 'discourse of power'. The more so inasmuch as he insists that the principal characteristic of power is always to manifest itself in a discourse about *something other*; power can only be effective—and tolerated—when some part of it is hidden. Power, it seems, has a capacity of infinite displacement; accordingly, it can only be caught 'on the wing', analysed in the places it both inhabits and vacates simultaneously, and hence viewed only indirectly. But sexuality is the place to grasp it most effectively, for the discourse on sexuality, actively promoted by the 'apparatus of power' (*dispositif du pouvoir*) in modern Western society, gives access to the human body and, through the body, to the control of the group, the species, and, finally, life itself.

The third way in which this book differs from others by Foucault is in the radicalism of its attack on 'knowledge' in all its forms. The studies of madness, clinical medicine, the human sciences, even that of 'the archaeology of knowledge', had continued to suggest that there was *some* ground, consisting perhaps of a theory of discourse itself, which might be used as a staging area for some positive conception of knowledge. Hope for the discovery of this ground is now realized. Everything is seen to consist in 'power', but power itself is viewed as indeterminable. Even the 'discourse about discourse' offers only an indirect insight into its nature. No sooner is power fixed in a 'meta-discourse' than it 'slips' to another domain, perhaps even to that of 'meta-discourse' itself. When knowledge is conceived to be so saturated with power that it is no longer distinguishable from it, the only recourse left is to a kind of power that eschews knowledge of every sort. The nature of such a power is only hinted at here, in Foucault's designation of the 'base' for a counter-attack against the 'apparatus of sexuality'. This base will be 'the body and pleasures'. How this base is to be constituted, however, is not made clear.

Finally, this work differs from others in Foucault's corpus by virtue of its overtly political tone and open orientation towards contemporary political questions. The same apocalyptical mood colours the end of the work; intimations of future biological wars and racial holocausts abound. But the dreams of a 'garden of delights', of 'good sex on the morrow', to be brought about by 'speaking out against the powers that be, telling the truth and promising enjoyment', all this is dismissed as fatuous utopianism. In fact, Foucault argues, such dreams confirm, when they are not complicit in, a 'discourse of sexuality' which exercises control and contributes to the massive process of 'normalization', precisely in so far as they credit the myth of 'repression' promoted by that discourse itself. Whence the twofold purpose of the proposed history of sexuality: to dissipate the myth of the repressive nature of modern society and to expose the operations of the *'dispositif du pouvoir'* in the very 'knowledge' which claims to liberate us from the effects of this repression.

The paradoxical opening we have come to expect in Foucault's discourse is not lacking in *The History of Sexuality*. It consists of the argument that, far from being sexually repressive, modern Western society, even in its Victorian golden age of repression, was anything but that; on the contrary, modern Western society has not only promoted more talk about sex, more study of it, more classifications of its forms, more theories of its processes than any culture known to human history; it has promoted as well the radical diversification of sexual practices, refined the forms that sexual desire and gratification may take, and accorded to 'sex' a greater metaphysical function than any other culture we know. The true originality of Western society in world culture, we might conclude, consists of its recognition that the promotion and control of the various forms of sexuality offer the best means of 'policing' society, of 'disciplining' human beings, and even of turning their 'perversions' to socially useful, i.e., power-serving, purposes.

Although the origins of this attitude towards sex are to be found in the Middle Ages, the 'break' in a generally healthy attitude towards the body and its functions occurs in the eighteenth century. At this time, sex becomes subject to causal and quantitative analyses, a matter of concern to the State, and a resource to be 'policed'—because it is perceived that sexual practices are the key to population control and therewith to 'wealth'. For the first time, at least in a significant way, 'how people use sex becomes a concern of society.' In the nineteenth century, the control of sex is effected by means of a movement both political and scientific, in which a sexual norm ('heterosexual monogamy') is constituted against which any form of sexuality that threatens the norm can be designated as *contre nature*'. Thus is created—and this is more important for an understanding of modern society than 'repression'—'the world of perversion'.

This world is the place where 'unnatural acts' are performed, and it is populated by a host of 'anti-social' types whose activities threaten the purity and health of the species: the sodomite, the onanist, the necrophiliac, the homosexual, the sadist, the masochist, and so on. But while being exiled to the confines of 'proper society', the inhabitants of this world are simultaneously discovered, by doctors, psychiatrists, preachers, teachers, and moralists in general, to reside also within the 'normal' family as well, as a threat to its 'health' and to the family's proper service to the 'race'. 'Perversion' is now contained within the body of the 'normal' person as a potentiality which must be identified, treated, disciplined, guarded against—in a ceaseless exercise of self-examination, confession, (psycho)analysis, regimentation, and general vigilance that ceases only with death. In fact, not surprisingly, the modern *scientia sexualis*, which takes shape over against general medicine on the one side and the ancient *ars erotica* on the other, even succeeds in finding death, in the form of the 'death wish', to underlie sexuality in general.

The great invention of this 'science' is nothing other than sexuality itself. It discovers, *before* sex and *beneath* it, the play of a 'force' which is 'everywhere' and 'nowhere', a process which is pathological in essence and a 'field of significations calling for decipherment', and a mechanism which, while localizable, is yet governed by indefinite causal connections. And the 'science of sex' makes of this force the 'secret', not only of life, but of the 'individual subject' as well. By its success in making the individual and the group seek their 'essence' and 'impurity' in real or imagined 'perversions', this 'science' (which includes even that 'liberating' discipline, psychoanalysis) serves a power which is only temporarily identifiable in class terms. Ultimately, Foucault predicts, it will serve to organize the wars of the races, each of which will see in sex a capital resource to be used in the 'bio-politics' of the future.

But the theory, or rather the myth, of repression has its golden age and perfect ground of cultivation in the era of the bourgeois family; for during this era 'science' identifies, and in the process brings into being, four specific social types which are generalized into the possible types that 'normal' humanity may incarnate: the hysterical woman, the masturbatory child, the perverse adult, and the Malthusian couple. The family is simultaneously defined as the 'normal' human unit and as the battleground (between men and women, young and old, parents and children, and, by extension, teachers and students, priests and laymen, rulers and ruled) where the prize to be won and the weapons to be used consist of the same thing: sexuality. 'Science', in seeking to control this battle, evolves four great strategies: the transformation of the body of the 'hysterical' woman into a medical object; of the sex of the infant into an educational object; of perverse pleasures into a psychiatric phenomenon; and of procreative conduct into an object for social control. These strategies have the effect of 'producing sexuality', and bringing under general social control the unit in which sexuality has its greatest play: the family. A whole apparatus is created for dealing with nothing but the problems which sexuality, now generalized and deemed eminently effective in the long run, creates in the family. 'Love' in the family is always under the threat of falling into 'perversion'; perversion in turn is linked to 'degeneracy', and degeneracy to loss of 'racial' power, wealth, status.

What Foucault purports to show, then, is that the 'theory of repression', far from being an instrument of liberation, is in fact a weapon used in the extension of social disciplining over every individual and group. And why this 'will to discipline'? Modern society apparently knows clearly what the individual only dimly grasps: that 'modern man is an animal whose politics brings his status as a living being into question'. The 'disciplines' not only know this, they 'prove' it; they provide the theory of an 'anatomo-politics of the human body' and of a 'bio-politics of the population'. In modern global warfare, Foucault concludes, it is no longer a matter of 'rights' that is at issue, but of 'life' itself. Since sex provides access to the 'life of the body and the life of the species', it functions in these sciences as both 'unique signifier' and 'universal signified' so convincingly that these sciences have succeeded, more completely than any *ars erotica* could ever do, in making 'sex itself desirable'.

Thus, the discourse on sexuality is shown simultaneously to reveal and to conceal the play of power in modern society and culture. Measured against the enormity of the power of this discourse, Foucault tells us, the manifestly 'political' discourses of the traditional ideologies pale to insignificance. Even the Nazis look tame in comparison with the 'bio-politics' which Foucault sees taking shape on the horizon. He foresees an era of racial wars made more virulent than anything previously known in the degree to which 'knowledge' will have succeeded in internalizing, within the individual and the group, the play of a 'sexuality' intended solely to discipline 'bodies and pleasures'.

Thus, Foucault's coming books promise to be even more apocalyptical than his earlier ones, in part because he has now come on his true subject: power. And power has been hypostatized, and given the status that spirit once enjoyed in an earlier, humanistic dispensation. Of course, his real subject had always been power, but power specified, located in particular exchanges between words and things. Now the 'void' out of which language was originally conceived to have spun its fictions has been filled. No void, but a plenum of force; not divine, but demonic. And the whole of culture, far from being that exercise of endless sublimation which humanism conceives to be the essence of our humanity, is revealed as nothing but repression. More or less killing, to be sure, but in the end nothing but destructive.

Summarized in this way, Foucault's work must seem to be little more than a continuation of a tradition of pessimistic, even decadent thought of which Schopenhauer, Gobineau, Nordau, and Spengler are representative. And it is true that he not only finds little to lament in the passing of Western civilization, he offers less hope for its replacement by anything better. But philosophers are under no obligation to be optimists, and neither are cultural commentators. The issue is not whether a thinker is an optimist or a pessimist, but the grounds for his point of view.

Foucault's grounds are difficult to specify, because he rejects most of the strategies of explanation which analysts of culture and history have honoured as legitimate bases for praising or condemning social practices in the past. At the centre of his thought is a theory of discourse based upon a rather conventional conception of the relation between language and experience, a theory originating in the now discredited discipline of rhetoric. Foucault uses rhetorical notions of language to project a conception of culture as magical, spectral, delusory. Strangely enough, this idea of language remains unexamined by him. In fact, although his thought is based primarily on a theory of language, he has not elaborated such a theory systematically. And as long as he fails to elaborate it, his thought remains captive to that very power which it has been his aim to dissipate.

Bibliography

Michel Foucault was born in 1926. After teaching philosophy at the University of Clermont-Ferrand he moved to Paris, and since 1970 he has been Professor of the History of Systems of Thought at the Collège de France.

BOOKS

Maladie mentale et psychologie (Paris, 1954)

Histoire de la folie (Paris, 1961); English translation, *Madness and Civilization: A History of Insanity in the Age of Reason* (London, 1971; New York, 1973)

Naissance de la clinique (Paris, 1963); English translation, *The Birth of the Clinic: An Archaeology of Medical Perception* (London and New York, 1973)

Raymond Roussel (Paris, 1963)

Les Mots et les choses: une archéologie des sciences humaines (Paris, 1966); English translation, *The Order of Things: An Archaeology of the Human Sciences* (New York, 1970; London, 1974)

L'Archéologie du savoir (Paris, 1969); English translation, *The Archaeology of Knowledge* (New York, 1972; London, 1974)

L'Ordre du discours (Paris, 1971); English translation, 'The Discourse on Language', included as appendix to *The Archaeology of Knowledge* (see above) (with Claudine Barret-Kriegel and others) '*Moi, Pierre Rivière, ayant égorgé ma mère, ma soeur et mon frère . . .': Un cas de parricide au XIXe siècle* (Paris, 1973); English translation, *'I, Pierre Rivière, Having Slaughtered My Mother, My Sister and My Brother . . .'* (London, 1978)

Surveiller et punir: Naissance de la prison (Paris, 1975); English translation, *Discipline and Punish: The Birth of the Prison* (London, 1977; New York, 1978)

Histoire de la sexualité, vol. I: *La volonté de savoir* (Paris 1976); English translation, *The History of Sexuality*, vol. I (New York, 1978; London, 1979)

Language, Counter-Memory, Practice, ed. D. F. Bouchard (Ithaca, N.Y., 1977; Oxford, 1978): an English translation of selected essays and interviews

Jacques Lacan

MALCOLM BOWIE

A lingering Romantic conception of genius leads us to expect of an original thinker that his ideas will spring in fully formed splendour from within himself, or from nature, or from nowhere. Where lesser minds may find proper employment in reading and elaborating texts from the past, the true innovator is expected to do everything for himself. Guided by an assumption of this kind, we may be embarrassed by thinkers who present themselves proudly as the readers and explainers of existing intellectual monuments. But evidence is plentiful to suggest that thinking done in the shadow of an admired predecessor may be thinking of great originality and strength. Plotinus reads Plato; Maimonides reads Aristotle; Averroës reads both; the young Marx reads Hegel. Assessing originality in such cases involves more work than we are perhaps accustomed to: the achievement of each later thinker may be well understood only if we are prepared to return to the works of the earlier and trace in detail the transformations and creative distortions they have undergone. Yet an investigation of this kind may be exhilarating: it may alert us not only to those ways of being original which our modern pieties overlook but to the large part which *re*thinking and *re*writing play even in the works of those who acknowledge no forebears and present themselves as exceptions to all rules but their own.

Lacan reads Freud. This is the simplest and most important thing about him. But where his forty-year exploration of Freud's works differs from the celebrated readings I have already mentioned is in the apparent purity of his motives. Where others have sought either to confront one body of ideas with another (Aristotle meets Islamic philosophy in the works of Averroës and rabbinic

Judaism in those of Maimonides) or to elaborate one strain of the original corpus in preference to others (Plotinus dwells upon the metaphysical and would-be mystical Plato), Lacan presents his main task as that of reading Freud well and getting him right.

That 'return to Freud' which he has proclaimed as his personal mission and slogan follows two distinct paths. The first and more straightforward operation is that of disinterring Freud's ideas from the litter of banalizing glosses and explanations which later writers have heaped upon them. And in the strenuous polemical activity which this involves Lacan's main . target is the international psychoanalytical movement itself; those for whom Freudian notions have mere commodity value—the sub-academic paperback-writer or the radical-chic conversationalist, for instance—are undeserving even of an incidental jibe. Most later psychoanalysts have done worse than misunderstand Freud: they have lost all sense of the weight, the perplexingness and the innovative power of Freud's ideas as they were first formulated by him. Those ideas have been all too superficially learnt and repeated, and adhered to with such childlike credence that they form a barrier rather than an inducement to the scientific investigation of mental process.

The procedures of initiation into psychoanalysis by which Freud sought to guarantee the continuity of his teaching often produce a disabling side-effect: 'Have these forms not led to a dispiriting formalism that discourages initiative by penalizing risk, and turns the reign of the opinion of the learned into a principle of docile prudence in which the authenticity of research is blunted [*s'émousse*] before it finally dries up?' (*Écrits*). In Lacan's writings psychoanalysis is repeatedly made to turn back upon itself and to re-examine its concepts, rituals, and institutions from the vantage-point offered by its own discoveries in their original unsystematized state.

The second and more complex operation involves Lacan in a greater risk than that of making enemies among his professional associates. For he sets out to correct certain parts of the Freudian corpus by reference to others. The discovery which Lacan places at the centre of Freud's achievement, and uses as his own essential conceptual tool in this correcting of Freud from within, is that of the unconscious—the unconscious which appears as an independent system, opposed to the 'preconscious–conscious' system,[1] in the second of Freud's major models of the psychical apparatus. (In the first, the 'Project for a Scientific Psychology' of 1895, the concept makes only the sketchiest of appearances; in the third—the triad comprising Id, Ego, and Superego introduced in 1923—it has a new and complex role: the main characteristics of the unconscious reappear in descriptions of the Id, but the Ego and the Superego are also held to have unconscious portions.) This version of the unconscious dominates Freud's thinking in the great creative phase which extends from *The Interpretation of Dreams* to the metapsychological papers of 1915. It is at once a topographical and a dynamic concept and, in the papers on 'Repression' and 'The Unconscious', is placed at the centre of Freud's most complex accounts of mental functioning.

For Lacan, as for many writers, Freud's essential insight was not—clearly not—that the unconscious exists, but that it has structure, that this structure affects in innumerable ways what we say and do, and that in thus betraying itself it becomes accessible to analysis. The unconscious as presented in *The Interpretation of Dreams*, *The Psychopathology of Everyday Life* and *Jokes and their Relation to the Unconscious* is endlessly voluble and self-revealing: in our dreams, forgettings, misrememberings, slips of tongue or pen, jokes, symptoms, verbal and physical mannerisms, it insists on being heard. The psychical energy by which repression takes place, and is maintained, is met and challenged by another energy which seeks, largely by means of dissimulation and subterfuge, to propel the repressed contents of the unconscious into the preconscious–conscious domain. The unending dialectic which this conflict produces exercises a special fascination upon Lacan's imagination, and his use of figurative language is never more forcible than when he depicts the unconscious speaking in the face

---

[1] 'As a substantive, it [the preconscious] denotes a system of the psychical apparatus that is quite distinct from the unconscious system; as an adjective it qualifies the operations and contents of this preconscious system. As these are not currently present in the field of consciousness, they are unconscious in the "descriptive" sense of the term, but they differ from the contents of the unconscious system in that they are in principle still accessible to consciousness (e.g. knowledge and memories that are not presently conscious)' (J. Laplanche and J.-B. Pontalis, *The Language of Psychoanalysis*). In psychoanalysis, the preconscious and the conscious are commonly considered as one continuous system, sharply distinguishable from the unconscious system.

of repression and censorship. In the following passage, for example, he extends and alters Plato's allegory of the cave:[2]

The locality in question is the entrance to the very cave in which Plato is known to guide us towards the exit, whereas people imagine they see the psychoanalyst going in. But things are less simple because this is an entrance which you never reach until the moment they're about to close (this locality will never attract the tourists), and because the only way of getting it to open up is to call out from the inside.

(*Écrits*)

Whenever we arrive at the cave of the unconscious, it is always closing time; the only way we have of gaining access is to be inside already. The structure of the unconscious is knowable only by those who are prepared to admit and espouse its inexhaustible capacity for displacement.[3]

Lacan, in his many attempts to re-teach psychoanalysis the provocativeness of its own insights, points to the insistent power of repression as it is exercised both within the analytic process and within the abstract working out of analytic theory. The discovery of the unconscious is itself subject to repression: the unconscious which, according to the very definitions on which psychoanalysis is founded, is the realm of free instinctual energy and knows no stability, or containment, or closure, is immobilized and domesticated by its professional observers. This extraordinary agent of dispersal and surprise becomes an ordinary counter within an ordinary conceptual game.

But the stultification of the unconscious message by post-Freudian analysts has its counterpart within Freud's own works. For Freud's discovery was a terrifying one, and his vision of endlessly proliferating and self-enmeshing psychical structure drove him to seek consolation in the cushioned world of mythical and metaphysical speculation. But although Freud lapsed from his own discovery in ways which his discovery should have allowed

[2] In Book VII of *The Republic* Plato compares mankind caught within the world of appearance to a prisoner in an underground cave. The prisoner's attempt to escape from the cave corresponds to man's quest for enlightenment and wisdom.

[3] Displacement: 'the fact that an idea's emphasis, interest or intensity is liable to be detached from it and to pass on to other ideas, which were originally of little intensity but which are related to the first idea by a chain of associations' (Laplanche and Pontalis, *op. cit.*).

him to foresee, his intellectual adventure is exemplary in the very dangers to which he succumbed: Lacan presents him as a new Actaeon turned upon and savaged by his own thoughts for having unveiled the goddess of the unconscious. Lacan's self-appointed task is to keep on thinking the intolerable Freudian thought, even at the price of dismemberment, and to allow repressed doctrine to make its disruptive return to psychoanalysis as it is performed and thought. Already we can begin to see how paradoxical Lacan's 'return to Freud' is, and how much disobedience this view of true loyalty might entail.

In Lacan's re-thinking of Freud's texts 'from within', the temptations of complete assent and complete dissent are refused with equal consistency. The beginnings of this tension are evident in Lacan's first major publication, *De la psychose paranoïaque dans ses rapports avec la personnalité* (1932; reprinted 1975). Lacan came to psychoanalysis by way of medicine and psychiatry, and this work, which was his doctoral dissertation, marks a crucial point of transition in his intellectual biography. While observing all the scholarly niceties which the format traditionally requires, he mounts an energetic attack on several dominant modes of psychiatric explanation. The study of paranoia has been impeded by the power which established psychiatry possesses to sanctify feeble or scantily tested hypotheses and turn them into dogma. Those who explain paranoia by reference to its supposed organic basis, or to the inherited disposition or 'constitutional type' of the patient, are resorting to an endlessly re-applicable interpretative trick which allows them to avoid acknowledging the complexity of individual human subjects.

Psychoanalysis offers Lacan a precious means of redirecting attention upon the paranoiac as *person*. Paranoia, no less than the neuroses around which psychoanalytic theory had been developed, may be coherently described and analysed by reference to the personality of the sufferer, his sexuality, childhood experiences, emotional development, family relationships, intellectual capacities and wishes for himself. Once this material has been collected and organized, no further point is served by inserting the patient into a pre-existing clinical typology or 'characterology'. Under the inspiration of psychoanalysis, Lacan is able to envisage a science of personality in which the subject retains his past, his intentions, and his creative intelligence. But even while drawing this lesson and acclaiming the 'immense genius of the master of psychoanalysis', Lacan stresses the limits of his debt and draws attention to confusions within Freud's theory. Moreover, and again characteristically, he draws on the work of other thinkers, including Spinoza, William James, Bergson, and Russell, in order to keep his own theoretical model permeable by other systems of thought. In the fierce argumentation of *De la psychose paranoïaque*, and in its array of fluid and mutually correcting concepts, an astonishing intellectual style has been created.

When Lacan read a paper introducing his notion of the 'mirror phase' to the International Psychoanalytical Congress held at Marienbad in 1936—and in so doing made his formal entry into the movement—he began to explore a mode of verbal production-in-performance which has remained peculiarly his. The bulk of his work since then has taken the form of conference papers and reports delivered to professional bodies; these are improvised from notes, reworked from transcript for publication, and often edited and annotated on subsequent appearances. A copious selection of these papers appeared as *Écrits* in 1966. They bear the marks both of that free association which psychoanalysis enjoins upon the patient as he speaks and of that 'evenly suspended attention' with which the analyst is expected to listen to the patient's words; this means that even Lacan's main ideas and cherished controversial positions are presented to the reader in a consciously ragged and inconsequential form.

The edited transcripts of the weekly seminars which Lacan conducts in Paris, now in process of publication, take us even further into his speculative workshop. Certain sections of the *Séminaire* serve to clarify the main ideas of *Écrits*, others elaborately rework them, and others still are the record of a surging glossolalia in the face of which critical intelligence falls indignantly or admiringly silent. Lacan's prose aspires perpetually to the condition of speech. And his aims in writing like this are clear: to allow the energies of the unconscious to become palpable in the wayward rhythm of his sentences, to discourage the reader from building premature theoretical constructions upon the text and to compel him to collaborate fully in the inventive work of language.

This characteristic of Lacan's writing makes his contributions to the technical vocabulary of psychoanalysis particularly difficult to summarize. For the terms and concepts with which he has extended and re-modelled Freud's are simply not available to us in a stable and circumscribed form. They define each other as they perform analytic work and undergo severe changes of implication as their intellectual context alters. Lacan is a builder of loosely moored conceptual mobiles in response to which the question 'What does this mean?' is better asked of a given term in the form 'What does it do?' or 'What paths does it travel?'. Moreover all Lacan's concepts, whatever main or subordinate part they play within his psychical models (or 'topologies' as he often calls them), serve too as polemical weapons: no account of them is complete without saying something about the ways in which they are adaptable to the changing needs of argument within his profession.

Consider, for example, the concept of the 'mirror phase' to which I have already referred. This phase occurs in the human individual between the ages of six months and eighteen months. It is a period at which, despite his imperfect control over his own bodily activities, he is first able to imagine himself as a coherent and self-governing entity. Such an image is concretely available to him when he sees his own reflection in a mirror:

This jubilant assumption of his specular image by the child at the *infans* stage, still sunk in his motor incapacity and nursling dependence, would seem to exhibit in an exemplary situation the symbolic matrix in which the *I* is precipitated in a primordial form, before it is objectified in the dialectic of identification with the other, and before language restores to it, in the universal, its function as subject.

(ibid.)

This moment of self-identification is crucial, however, not because it represents a stage on the way towards 'adulthood' or 'genital maturity'—such developmental models of the changing human subject come under constant attack from Lacan—but because it represents a permanent tendency of the individual: the tendency which leads him throughout life to seek and foster the imaginary wholeness of an 'ideal ego'. The unity invented at these moments, and the ego which is the product of successive inventions, are both spurious; they are attempts to find ways round certain inescapable factors of lack (*manque*), absence and incompleteness in human living.

Even in my few lines of quotation and summary it is plain that Lacan's concept of the mirror phase reaches far beyond the confines of child psychology for its fullest validation. Towards the end of the passage a theory of language and a theory of interpersonal perception are taking shape; another order of experience is emerging over and against the order of imaginary identifications which the 'specular' moment inaugurates; and one of Lacan's favourite objections to psychoanalysis as traditionally practised may already be glimpsed: if the ego is no more than an imaginary precipitate, how absurd it is for the proponents of 'ego psychology' to appoint themselves to the task of developing and stabilizing that ghostly entity.

In a sense all complex conceptual systems work like this, with each component helping to define and activate the others. But where these systems are customarily divided by their authors into separately tractable sub-units, it is for Lacan a matter of personal scruple that no such division should take place. Every concept acts as a nodal point within a network of choices and refusals, and is presented to the reader in a language where the practical business of choosing and refusing remains present as a syntactic turmoil.

I shall now turn to that central series of insights and conjectures about the structure of the unconscious upon which Lacan's entire theory of psychical process is founded. For his characteristic and much-publicized modes of thinking, talking, and writing make their fullest sense, and offer themselves to responsible judgement, only when considered in the context of this theory.

In Freud's central account of the unconscious a series of topographical dynamic and economic models[4] are fused. His discovery was not of the sort that could be declared and developed in a single, ready-made theoretical language. When, after many years of analytic practice and speculation, he came to list the characteristics of the unconscious as a system, he was still using a technical vocabulary to which biology, mechanics, logic, and language study had each made a distinctive contribution. The unconscious, he claimed, has at its core a set of instinctual impulses which are able to coexist without mutual influence or contradiction; it knows

[4] For the distinctions between models of these three kinds, see Laplanche and Pontalis, *op. cit.*

no negation, no doubt, no degrees of certainty; it is the realm of the primary process, in which psychical energy is freely transmissible between ideas by means of displacement and condensation;[5] it is timeless; it is concerned not with external reality but with the achievement of pleasure and the corresponding avoidance of unpleasure.

A main intuition of Lacan's was that Freud's account of the unconscious and its relations with the preconscious–conscious system could be reorganized around a relatively small number of linguistic concepts, and thereby be made at once more cogent and more elastic. The cue for this innovation was provided by Freud himself, in whose works 'facts of language' are given extraordinary prominence. In analysing the verbal narratives which provided the central fund of evidence for his case-histories and his books on dreams, verbal and other slips, and jokes, he shows much skill and delicacy as a textual critic. The developing functions of human language are a theme particularly dear to him. The linguistic sciences are often called upon to provide analogies and corroborative evidence in his psychological writings. That Freud himself had not drawn to any appreciable extent upon linguistics proper is, for Lacan, a matter of historical chance: the foundations of that discipline were being laid by Saussure and others at the same time as Freud's theory was being constructed, and he could not have been expected to have detailed knowledge of, or draw useful inferences from, a neighbouring science *in statu nascendi*.

The lessons which the accident of birth made Freud unable, and Lacan able, to learn are principally those concerning the synchronic analysis of complex systems. Comparative philology, which was still monarch of the linguistic sciences during Freud's formative years, not only had little to teach about such analysis but was sometimes, for the psychologist, a positive encouragement to error. In reviewing Karl Abel's conjectural and now discredited pamphlet on *The Antithetical Meaning of Primal Words* (1884), for example, Freud drew a parallel between the dreaming mind, which knows no contradiction, and a primitive state of human language postulated by Abel in which certain words had had

---

[5] '[Condensation is] ... one of the essential modes of the functioning of the unconscious processes: a sole idea represents several associative chains at whose point of intersection it is located' (ibid.).

opposite meanings at once. (Old English *bat* ('good') and *badde* ('bad') are assumed to derive from a common ancestor meaning 'good-bad'.) Freud later used Abel's work as his sole support for the view that 'the equivalence of contraries in dreams is a universal archaic trait in human thinking'. He had, that is to say, based a characteristic wishful fantasy about 'the origin of things' upon a piece of fairy-tale philology.

Linguistics, on the other hand, inhibits this kind of speculation and suggests a more productive mode of comparison between language and mind. In so far as it studies the minimal differential units which constitute language, and the ways in which those units may be embraced and interrelated within comprehensive systems, it provides a series of testable models for the psychical apparatus. Where philology took Freud into a whimsical no-man's-land, linguistics, as manipulated by Lacan, could return psychoanalysis to the tasks Freud was best at: the working out and the coherent articulation of mental structure.

'L'inconscient est structuré comme un langage' (The unconscious is structured like a language). This best-known of Lacan's pronouncements makes plain the importance of his debt to linguistics; and, having the form of a simile, it serves as a reminder of the problems which the recourse to linguistic concepts raises for psychoanalysis. The first questions we are likely to ask of Lacan's formula are: how exact and how useful are analogies of this kind? Does the first term take logical priority over the second? Would the same thing, or a different but equally interesting thing, or a lesser thing, be said if the order of the terms were reversed? Lacan's work in this area is a sequence of two-way mappings—of the unconscious upon language and of language upon the unconscious—performed in such sustained defiance of his reader's wish for firm landmarks that these first questions are never definitively answered.

The relationship between language and the unconscious may be looked at broadly in two ways. First, it is clearly possible that psychical tensions and conflicts could have played their part in determining the structure of human language in the first place: the idea that language was created in the partial image of the unconscious offers at the very least an appealing poetic explanation for that sense of a natural interlocking between the two systems which students of the unconscious report. Secondly, language is the sole medium of psychoanalysis: for the patient as he speaks his dreams and his fantasies, and for the analyst as he punctuates the patient's discourse and places constructions upon it, the unconscious is available only in a linguistically mediated form. There is no point in speculating about a possible 'pure', pre-linguistic state of the unconscious, nor in seeking to describe the ways in which the observational instrument of language may imprint its own structures upon the unconscious materials observed. For language is the medium of these secondary investigations too, and having 'tricked' us once will trick us again.

Lacan has little patience with the first approach, and is inclined to put matters the other way round: language creates the unconscious. And he sees linguistic mediation as extending far beyond the analytic dialogue. He points out that the human subject, as he acquires speech, is inserting himself into a pre-existing symbolic order and thereby submitting his libido (*désir*) to the systemic pressures of that order: in adopting language he allows his free instinctual energies to be operated upon and organized. It is the peculiar privilege of man the language-user to remain oblivious, while making things with words, of the extent to which words have made, and continue to make, him.

Lacan's comparison of language and the unconscious as entire systems, and his account of their many possible reciprocities, are supported by detailed work on the elementary structural components of each. He draws in particular upon Saussure's binomial definition of the linguistic sign—signifier (*signifiant*) and signified (*signifié*) in arbitrary association—and on the metaphoric and metonymic poles of verbal organization proposed by the linguist Roman Jakobson. (I shall discuss both these sets of terms in a moment.) These concepts are useful for a number of reasons: because they correspond neatly to certain antithetical pairs of concepts within Freud's thinking; because they are readily combinable and permutable within the pseudo-algebraic representations of mental process which Lacan has come increasingly to favour; and because a severe limitation is placed on the larger act of comparison. The limitation is simply this: that there is very little in Freud's presentation of the unconscious which corresponds to the sentence, or to syntactic structure in general. Indeed much of .

the surprising originality which Freud ascribes to the unconscious stems from its refusal of allegiance to exactly those modes of hierarchical organization which syntax promotes. The system of a given language as articulated in its grammar could therefore have only a small role in psychoanalytic accounts of mental functioning. Rather than use an ill-adapted set of grammatical categories, Lacan chose to base his models on certain underlying binary structures with a high capacity for recombination.

This application to psychoanalysis of Saussure's teachings received its first full expression in the papers 'The Function and Field of Speech and Language in Psychoanalysis' and 'The Agency of the Letter in the Unconscious or Reason since Freud', delivered in 1953 and 1957 respectively. But Lacan does not import a stable linguistic theory into psychoanalysis with a view to bringing a still unruly body of doctrine to order: the encounter between Freud and Saussure will allow each to become re-thinkable in the light of the other.

For Saussure the sign represented a sudden collision and bonding between two distinct realms, each of which was in itself fluid and undifferentiated: thought on the one hand and the sound of the human voice on the other. But once bonding has taken place between a segment of the thought-realm (a signified) and a segment of the sound-realm (a signifier) their relationship is intimate to the point of complete interdependence:

Again language is comparable to a sheet of paper: thought is the front and sound is the back; you cannot cut up the front without at the same time cutting up the back; similarly, in language you cannot isolate sound from thought, nor thought from sound; you could only manage to do this by a process of abstraction which would result in the creation of pure psychology or pure phonology.

(*Course in General Linguistics*)

What Lacan questions, even as he borrows the Saussurian terminology, is the state of symmetry and equilibrium between signifier and signified which is described in passages such as this. He uses the formulation $\frac{S}{s}$ (signifier over signified) not only as a minimal summary of Saussure's theory, but as a way of highlighting a stubborn problem within it: the exact status and role of the signified. To this latter end, Lacan treats the algorithm $\frac{S}{s}$, which seems at first glance no more than an operational procedure within a calculus of his own devising, as a concrete poem and a personal emblem. For the bar separating the two symbols is itself more than a symbol: it is the pictorial enactment of a necessary and irremoveable cleavage between them. Similarly, the placing *beneath* of the signified is more than a matter of mathematical convention and convenience. For the signified does indeed, in Lacan's account, 'slip beneath' the signifier and successfully resist our attempts to locate and delimit it. The supremacy of the signifier (capital letter, roman type, upper position) over the signified (small letter, italic type, lower position) is made visible before us.

The burden of Lacan's argument is that the quest for the signified in its 'pure' form—the quest, that is to say, for the pristine, word-free structures of thought—is frivolous; language has a constitutive role in human thinking; 'pure psychology' of the kind invoked by Saussure does not exist. The proper object of attention, for the psychoanalyst no less than for the linguist, is the signifying chain itself: the relationships observable within that chain are the surest guide to psychical structure and to the structure of the human subject.

Once the kernel of Saussure's thought has been dramatized in this way, Lacan is able to use it as a means both of organizing and of de-stabilizing psychoanalytic theory. At first sight his undertaking looks dangerously restrictive. For the distinction between signifier and signified, in so far as it opposes the manifest to the latent, is adaptable in the extreme and may be assimilated in turn to a variety of distinctions which Freud himself had presented and manipulated separately: those, for example, between the conscious and the unconscious, between dream-images and 'latent dream thoughts', between neurotic symptoms and repressed wishes.

But in collapsing these pairs of antithetical categories into an all-purpose two-term code Lacan is not being lazy and is not falsely schematizing Freud's thought. The procedures for structural analysis which he follows as he examines the procession of variously connected signifiers are those which Freud had formulated in his accounts of the dreamwork. In this passage from *Jokes and Their Relation to the Unconscious*, for example, summarizing the notion of displacement, Freud gives a clear portrait of the signifier at play:

The dream-work ... exaggerates this method of indirect expression beyond all bounds. Under the pressure of the censorship, any sort of connection is good enough to serve as a substitute by allusion, and displacement is allowed from any element to any other. Replacement of internal associations (similarity, causal connection, etc.) by what are known as external ones (simultaneity in time, contiguity in space, similarity of sound) is quite especially striking and characteristic of the dream-work.

On countless occasions in his presentation of case material, Freud appears as the delighted observer of an unconscious which fulfils its wishes by an ingenious manipulation of extraneous and unwished-for materials. The difference of emphasis between Freud and Lacan is this: Freud, while acknowledging the power of his 'external associations', sees them as making their fullest sense only when measured against the 'internal associations' which they disguise or replace; dream-images require the conjectural 'latent dream thoughts' in order to become legible; the signified, even as it slips from view, invites pursuit. For Lacan this interpretative oscillation between signifier and signified can easily divert attention from the former and into a fluid region of wish-fulfilment fantasy; the relations between signifiers are a neglected resource and provide more than a sufficiency of information for the analyst.

Lacan's stress on the signifier and his winnowing of the structural from the hermeneutic components of Freud's theory entail a further excursion into the linguistic domain. His debt on this second occasion is to Jakobson, in whose two poles of verbal organization he saw the clue to two underlying and irreducible modes of connection within the signifying chain. For Jakobson the two poles, metaphoric and metonymic, coexist competitively within any symbolic process, and he himself drew attention to a possible overlap between his own categories and those used by Freud in characterizing the unconscious: Freud's 'displacement' and 'condensation' were both based on the principle of contiguity, the one being metonymic and the other synecdochic;[6] his 'identification' and 'symbolism' were based on similarity, and are hence metaphoric. Lacan pays no attention to this inelegant suggestion

[6] Metonymy: 'A figure in which the name of an attribute or adjunct is substituted for that of the thing meant'. Synecdoche: 'a figure by which a more comprehensive term is used for a less comprehensive or vice versa; as whole for part or part for whole, etc.' (*OED*).

of Jakobson's, and puts forward a simpler and more persuasive pair of equivalences: condensation (*Verdichtung*) corresponds to metaphor, and displacement (*Verschiebung*) to metonymy. These are Freud's crucial categories; identification and symbolism are easily converted into one or other of them.

But Lacan is not content to leave matters here, with each linguistic term brought into alignment with one mode of unconscious mental functioning. Jakobson's terms no less than Saussure's have a further test to pass: if they are to become what they describe, become signifiers in their own right, then they must show themselves to be multiple, overdetermined,[7] and permanently available for new uses. To this end, which is that of a continual new beginning, an additional pair of crosswise relationships is created: the psychical mechanism by which neurotic symptoms are produced involves the pairing of two signifiers—unconscious sexual trauma and changes within, or actions by, the body—and is thus metaphorical; whereas unconscious desire, indestructible and insatiable as it is, involves a constant displacement of energy from object to object and is thus metonymic. (An arrest of the metonymic function produces not a symptom but a fetish.)

The result of this double reshuffling of Jakobson's polarity is that the terms 'metaphor' and 'metonymy' not only introduce clear and useful subdivisions within the notion of signifier, but play an enigmatic signifying game of their own. The process is familiar throughout Lacan's work. His theoretical meta-language becomes, in its constant effort of adaptation to the unconscious, language pure and simple—which means language heterogeneous and complex: 'there is no meta-language . . . no language can say the truth about the truth, since the truth founds itself on the fact that it speaks and that it has no other means of doing so' (*Écrits*).

I suggested earlier that the very form in which the proposition 'The unconscious is structured like a language' is cast draws attention to its own possible limitations as a theoretical principle. But the ways in which Lacan manages to avoid these limitations should by now be clear. For questions of logical or chronological priority between

[7] Overdetermination: 'the fact that formations of the unconscious (symptoms, dreams, etc.) can be attributed to a plurality of determining factors' (Laplanche and Pontalis, op. cit.).

the unconscious and language begin to dissolve as soon as a 'symbolic order' embracing both is envisaged. Precisely by confining himself to the *fundamentals* of language as described by Saussure and Jakobson, rather than exploring the higher, syntactic modes of organization, Lacan keeps in contact with the elementary differential components of all symbolic systems. The unconscious, in so far as it becomes visible and audible in speech, symptoms, dreams and involuntary acts of omission or commission, is governed by the same rules as all other systems: the rules which Lacan has expressed in summary form as the 'law of the Signifier'. So confident is he that he has made contact here with something fundamental and universal, that he draws attention to an element of redundancy in his own phrase 'structured like a language': 'structured' and 'like a language' mean exactly the same thing. 'Il n'est structure que de langage' (There is no structure except of, or by means of, language).

The special role—variously called primacy, precedence, preeminence, insistence, supremacy—assigned by Lacan to the signifier in the psychical life is accompanied by another major redefinition of terms and another unremitting polemical campaign. I refer to the terms 'subject' (*sujet*) and 'ego' (*moi*). Whereas the ego, first glimpsed at the mirror stage, is the reified product of successive imaginary identifications and is cherished as the stable or would-be stable seat of personal 'identity', the subject is no *thing* at all and can be grasped only as a set of tensions, or mutations, or dialectical upheavals within a continuous, intentional, future-directed process. The ego as a tension-point within Freud's Id–Ego–Superego topography is respected by Lacan as a necessary component of a properly dialectical model of the human subject. But the ego envisaged as an end in itself, as a threatened residence of selfhood needing continually to be refortified against hostile incursions from the id and the superego, is treated with scorn: this stabilized and tranquillized ego plays dumbly into the hands of the 'soul-managers' and the social engineers. Lacan's accounts of the psychical apparatus at work have at their centre the notion not of ego but of subject. The subject does not 'disappear' in Lacan's hands, as a fashionable phrase would have it, but has its manifold trajectories plotted and re-plotted by him.

The basis for the mobility of the subject is supplied by the signifying chain itself. For the signifier not only constitutes and governs the subject—Lacan speaks of 'the supremacy of the signifier in the subject' and of 'the pre-eminence of the signifier over the subject'—but positively requires the subject as its mediating term: 'a signifier is that which represents the subject for another signifier'. Far from being a by-product or an epiphenomenon of the signifier, the subject has a relationship of interdependence with it, and to such an extent that whatever may be claimed for the one must needs be claimed, with appropriate modifications, for the other. Both are characterized by their power of indefinite structural displacement, and that power necessarily takes priority over all innate or acquired psychological characteristics:

> the displacement of the signifier determines the subjects in their acts, in their destiny, in their refusals, in their blindnesses, in their end and in their fate, their innate gifts and social acquisitions notwithstanding, without regard for character or sex, and . . . willingly or not, everything that might be considered the stuff of psychology, kit and caboodle, will follow the path of the signifier.
>
> (ibid.)

The traditional language of psychology has an inveterate tendency to describe the mind as if it were a stable collection of things, or forces, or faculties, and Lacan's presentation of the subject-in-process may at first seem impossibly flimsy and weightless to those whose expectations of coherence in psychical model-building have been conditioned by that language. What is remarkable is that his view of the subject as 'merely' empty, mobile, and without a centre should emerge, in its passage from one analytic task to the next, and through a language in which all expectations of coherence are indiscriminately dismantled, as at once cogent and precise.

Lacan calls the domain of the signifier, in which this perpetual restructuring of the subject takes place, the Symbolic order. And this order is the dominant one in the triad Symbolic–Imaginary–Real which has acquired a creative role in Lacan's thought comparable to that of Id–Ego–Superego in the later thought of Freud. (Although Lacan's three orders and Freud's three agencies are called upon to do the same sorts of analytic work, it would be impossible to establish a term-for-term equivalence between them.) Each of Lacan's orders is better thought of as a shifting gravitational centre for his arguments than as a stable concept; at any moment each may be implicated in the redefinition of the others.

I have already suggested something of the contrast between the Symbolic and the Imaginary in my remarks on the subject and the ego. Where the one is characterized by difference, disjunction, and displacement the other is a seeking for identity or resemblance. The Imaginary grows from the infant's experience of his 'specular ego' but extends far into the adult individual's experience of others and of the external world: wherever a false identification is to be found—within the subject, or between one subject and another, or between subject and thing—there the Imaginary holds sway. Although the two orders are distinct and opposed, the Symbolic encroaches upon the Imaginary, organizes it, and gives it direction; the false fixities of the Imaginary are exposed, and coerced into movement, by the signifying chain.

The Real is the most puzzling of the three, and is given much less attention than the others in *Écrits*; Lacan's *Séminaire* contains the fullest and most challenging accounts of it. Two apparently divergent general tendencies may be discerned in Lacan's presentation of this notion. First, the Real is that which is there, already there, and inaccessible to the subject, whether this be a physical object or a sexual trauma; when we appear on the scene as subjects certain games have already been played, certain dice thrown. Things *are*. But to become aware of this is not to be compelled to silent acquiescence: 'Don't you think there's something derisory and laughable in the fact that the dice have already been cast?' (*Séminaire*, II). The way beyond this 'laughable' Real is the uniquely human way offered by the Symbolic order: thanks to that order the dice may be thrown again. Secondly, however, the Real is the primordial chaos upon which language operates: 'It is the world of words that creates the world of things—the things originally confused in the *hic et nunc* of the all in the process of coming-into-being' (*Écrits*); the Real is given its structure by the human power to name.

Neither of these conceptions is at all original, and the language of common sense plays a prominent role in the presentation of each. And their divergence is only apparent. They place a common stress upon the limits of the linguistic power: the Real is that which is radically extrinsic to the procession of signifiers. The Real may be structured—'created' even—by the subject for himself, but it cannot be named. It is the irremediable and intractable 'outside' of language; the indefinitely receding goal towards which the signifying chain tends; the vanishing point of the Symbolic and Imaginary alike. As a result of this view, the Real comes close to meaning 'the ineffable' or 'the impossible' in Lacan's thought. As a term within the triad it has less work to do than the others. But it serves admirably both to re-introduce problems and asymmetries into what could easily have become a facile dualism between the Symbolic and the Imaginary, and to remind Lacan's would-be omnipotent subject that his symbolic and imaginary constructions take place in a world which exceeds him.

Lacan's account of the subject as 'decentred' and dialectical is itself reworked in numerous ways and systematically protected from the danger of promoting or seeming to promote an array of fixed and readily re-applicable concepts. Although there is no foolproof way for Lacan or anyone else to prevent conscientiously scattered doctrine from becoming centralized doctrine, or the resistance to cant from engendering cant of its own, his precautions have in general worked well. For the near-synonyms which he uses in depicting the discontinuous itineraries of the subject (*'refente'*, *'division'*, *'Spaltung'*, *'fading'*, and so forth) are kept in motion by a dominant polysemic term: 'the Other' (*l'Autre*). More consistently than any other of Lacan's terms 'the Other' refuses to yield a single sense; in each of its incarnations it is that which introduces 'lack' and 'gap' into the operations of the subject and which, in doing so, incapacitates the subject for selfhood, or inwardness, or apperception, or plenitude; it guarantees the indestructibility of desire by keeping the goals of desire in perpetual flight.

For Lacan as for Freud the primal Other is the father within the Oedipal triangle—who forbids incest, threatens castration, and, by placing an absolute prohibition upon the child's desire for its mother, becomes the inaugurating agent of Law. Lacan is concerned not with the real or imaginary fathers of a given individual but with the symbolic father whose name initiates and propels the signifying chain: 'It is in the *name of the father* [*nom du père*] that we must recognize the support of the symbolic function which, from the dawn of history, has identified his person with the figure of the law' (ibid.). The original encounter with the legislating *nom-du-père*, and the abiding lack and non-satisfaction to which the subject is thereby condemned, produce the complex pattern of inter-mingled aggression and subservience which is to mark the subject indelibly in his dealings with others. (Lacan makes frequent use of Hegel's dialectic of master and slave as an easily reconstruable model for this process.) These dealings, whether in the form of the everyday encounter between people or in that of the dialogue between patient and analyst, are a main concern of Lacan's, and he discusses with extraordinary insight their determining role in the constitution of the subject.

The subject is made and re-made in his encounter with the Other:

What I seek in speech is the response of the other. What constitutes me as subject is my question. In order to be recognized by the other, I utter what was only in view of what will be. In order to find him, I call him by a name that he must assume or refuse in order to reply to me.

It is from the Other that the subject receives even the message that he emits.

The Other is, therefore, the locus in which is constituted the I who speaks to him who hears, that which is said by the one being already the reply, the other deciding to hear it whether the one has or has not spoken.

(ibid.)

The relationship between Subject and Other is characterized by desire:

... man's desire finds its meaning in the desire of the other, not so much because the other holds the key to the object desired, as because the first object of desire is to be recognized by the other.

Indeed, it is quite simply ... as desire of the other that man's desire finds form.

... man's desire is the desire of the Other [*le désir de l'Autre*] in which the 'of' [*de*] provides what grammarians call the 'subjective determination', namely that it is *qua* Other that he desires (which is what provides the true compass of human passion).

(ibid.)

Much deliberate alteration of meaning is visible within and be-tween remarks such as these: the Other is, for example, now one term in the dialectical couple Subject–Other, now the entire locus or condition of 'otherness' (*altérité*, *hétéronomie*) which embraces both terms. And the picture is further complicated when the same term is used to bind the intrapersonal and interpersonal worlds together.

Freud's essential discovery, Lacan tells us, was that man bears otherness within him. The schism between the unconscious and the preconscious–conscious systems brings man face to face with his own radical 'extraneousness to himself'. When viewed from the vantage point of the preconscious–conscious, the unconscious—the signifying chain through which all desire passes—is another place and another language: 'l'inconscient, c'est le discours de l'Autre' (the unconscious is the discourse of the Other). The message which is passed across the gap between the subject and the external Other passes inwardly too: 'the unconscious is that discourse of the Other where the subject receives, in the inverted form which is appropriate to the promise, his own forgotten message'. Lest the Other as a concept become one-dimensional and inert despite Lacan's precautions, it is shadowed in his later thinking by the mysterious 'small-other object' ('objet *a*') which is, among many things, the imagined presence and the imagined absence of the phallus within the Oedipal triangle.

The reader of Lacan may find himself wondering about the credentials of a term which ranges so promiscuously between arguments: what is this 'Other' that it should be ennobled by a capital letter and so freely convertible? How can the term remain useful as an operational device when it may be variously defined as a father, a place, a point, any dialectical partner, a horizon within the subject, a horizon beyond the subject, the unconscious, language, the signifier? Could it be that the capital letter is employed to give an untidy *omnium gatherum* a false aura of authority?

The charge of intellectual irresponsibility which questions such as these seem about to make against Lacan is to a large extent forestalled if his thought is considered whole, and as a comprehensive system of mutually implying parts. For the *nom-du-père*, the original Other, introduces a gap between desire and its object(s) which the subject is bounded by, and bound to, throughout his life and at all levels of his experience. This primordial estrangement is by its very nature destined to recur, and be converted, ubiquitously; it is the origin of language and the subject alike, and provides an essential precondition for the humanity of man. And just as this first otherness travels freely between all human places and occasions, so the term 'Other' migrates and is converted within Lacan's prose. Lacan would claim no responsibility for the polysemy of his term; nothing could require him to be personally answerable for a fact of life. . . .

It will be clear from everything I have said so far that Lacan has given language a role of unprecedented importance within the field of psychoanalytic enquiry. In his pamphlet on *The Question of Lay Analysis*, Freud insisted that a future 'college of psychoanalysis' would not only teach disciplines familiar within medical faculties but 'would include branches of knowledge which are remote from medicine and which the doctor does not come across in his practice: the history of civilization, mythology, the psychology of religion and the science of literature. Unless he is well at home in these subjects, the analyst can make nothing of a large amount of his material.' Lacan's additions to this list include not only linguistics, but 'rhetoric, dialectic in the technical sense that this word assumes in the *Topics* of Aristotle, grammar, and, that supreme pinnacle of the aesthetics of language, poetics, which would include the neglected technique of the witticism [*mot d'esprit*]'. The analyst who brings these branches of learning to bear upon his work is not departing from tradition but returning to the fertile sources of psychoanalytic thinking: Freud and his early followers had an exemplary knowledge of, and responsiveness to, literature and the linguistic sciences.

Lacan's debt to linguistics has already been discussed. But three further debts in this area deserve to be mentioned: to rhetoric and stylistics, to critical exegesis, and to the practice of literary production at large. For the imprint which these activities have left on Lacan's work makes it peculiarly and problematically available to intruders from the world of letters, and gives us a series of major clues in any attempt to understand the extraordinary catalytic role which his thought has developed within the 'human sciences' in contemporary France.

In his references to the figures and tropes of classical rhetoric, Lacan adheres to a mode of speculative comparison much favoured by Freud. In the following paragraph from *The Claims of Psychoanalysis to Scientific Interest* (1913), for example, Freud, having discussed dreams as being 'like a language', moves on to another inventive analogy:

If we reflect that the means of representation in dreams are principally visual images and not words, we shall see that it is even more appropriate to compare dreams with a system of writing than with a language. In fact the interpretation of dreams is completely analogous to the decipherment of an ancient pictographic script such as Egyptian hieroglyphs. In both cases there are certain elements which are not intended to be interpreted (or read, as the case may be) but are only designed to serve as 'determinatives', that is to establish the meaning of some other element. The ambiguity of various elements of dreams finds a parallel in these ancient systems of writing; and so too does the omission of various relations, which have in both cases to be supplied from the context. If this conception of the method of representation in dreams has not yet been followed up, this, as will be readily understood, must be ascribed to the fact that psycho-analysts are entirely ignorant of the attitude and knowledge with which a philologist would approach such a problem as that presented by dreams.

The relationship between dreams and hieroglyphic script for Freud is identical with that between the mechanisms of the unconscious and rhetoric for Lacan:

Periphrasis, hyperbaton, ellipsis, suspension, anticipation, retraction, negation, digression, irony, these are the figures of style (Quintilian's *figurae sententiarum*); as catachresis, litotes, antonomasia, hypotyposis are the tropes whose terms suggest themselves as the most proper for the labelling of these mechanisms. Can one really see these as mere figures of speech when it is the figures themselves that are the active principle of the rhetoric of the discourse that the analysand in fact utters?

(*Écrits*)

For both writers the fascinating thing is not so much that comparisons of this kind are instructive as that terms apparently so remote from each other should be comparable at all. Hieroglyphics and rhetoric both represent the triumph of calculation and civilized artifice over the brute materials of experience. How strange, therefore, that the unconscious, so easily thought of as brutish and anarchic, should reveal itself to have a perfectly 'civilized' cunning in the ways it manipulates its structures.

As we have seen, Lacan gives two rhetorical terms—metaphor

and metonymy—special duties and privileges in his writing. But although many other terms are proclaimed in lists like the one I have just quoted, they are much more important for the lesson they teach corporately than for any individual uses they might have as analytic tools. The analyst who knows about rhetoric is more likely than a colleague who does not to remain alert both to those inflections of normal usage which comprise the 'style' and the singularity of an individual patient's discourse and to the specific characters of the unconscious discourse which the spoken word allows the analyst to reconstrue. The enduring appeal which comparisons like these hold for both Freud and Lacan stems from their combined universalizing and particularizing capacities: they serve to enforce a general truth about the unconscious—that it has, or, in Lacan's view, *is* structure—but at the same time allow the informed observer to focus sharply on the manner in which nameable individuals suffer.

Lacan's skill and resourcefulness as an exegete are visible throughout his writings. His command of the Freudian corpus and his ability to argue on many levels, and many sides of the question, at once are such that a great deal of exposition and commentary takes place between the lines: possible new senses for Freud's texts emerge in rapid succession as we read, and important reservations about certain of Freud's ideas, whether in their original or derived forms, may be glimpsed behind a sudden turmoil of parentheses, asides, or qualifying phrases. (Lacan presupposes a detailed knowledge of Freud in the colleagues or pupils who are his original hearers; the general reader of *Écrits* who is not so equipped will need unusual powers of imagination, or of self-deception, in order to make headway.) Nevertheless there are several occasions in *Écrits* and the *Séminaire* when texts are read and re-read with minute explicitness. Of these texts two prove to be especially revealing: a sentence by Freud and a short story by Edgar Allan Poe.

In the final sentences of the third of his *New Introductory Lectures*, Freud speaks of the continuing work of analysis: 'Where id was, there ego shall be. It is a work of culture—not unlike the draining of the Zuider Zee.' The penultimate sentence, which is 'Wo Es war, soll Ich werden' in the original, is given in the standard

French translation as 'Le Moi doit déloger le ça' (The ego must unseat the id). Lacan is vehement against this French version because it excludes levels of sense present in the original. Freud's is a gnomic utterance worthy of the Pre-Socratics. Lacan points out that Freud, contrary to his usual practice, does not use the forms 'das Es' and 'das Ich', and that by these omissions of the definite article two psychical agencies have become two universal principles; that the sentence is a moral imperative; that its two nouns are not flatly opposed; and that it contains an astonishing paradox: '[celui] d'un impératif qui me presse d'assumer ma propre causalité' ([that] of an imperative which urges me to assume my own causality). An entire range of paraphrases and 'improved' translations is provided:

Là où fut ça, il me faut advenir (*Écrits*).

Là où c'était, là comme sujet dois-je advenir (ibid.).

Là où c'était, peut-on dire, là où s'était, voudrions-nous faire qu'on entendît, c'est mon devoir que je vienne à être (ibid.).

Ici, dans le champ du rêve, tu es chez toi (*Séminaire*, XI).

Ainsi se ferme la voie imaginaire, par où je dois dans l'analyse advenir, là où s'était l'inconscient (*Écrits*).

Lacan contends in each of these reformulations that the realm of unconscious energy, far from requiring ever firmer custodianship and control from the ego, has unsuspected bounty to offer: it is the proper site for the subject, a repository of truth. The 'I' should take up residence there not as a coercive occupying force but as one who willingly casts aside falsehood and returns home; the prodigal 'I' becomes *subject* to the precise extent that it travels back to the unconscious and adopts its plural structures.

If considered solely in the context of Freud's lecture, Lacan's reading of the sentence would seem improbable: for the ego's need for mastery over the id is one of Freud's themes in earlier pages, and the erring French translator has given us the gist of a remark which aptly recapitulates that theme. Yet there is no reason why the remark should simply confirm what has gone before: elsewhere Freud had shown himself surprised and saddened by what he took to be a gratuitous urge to repression within the ego, and had sought ways of persuading it to relax its damagingly tight grip upon the id. It is quite possible that he was allowing the parting moral assertion of his lecture to echo these doubts. But what Lacan has done to the sentence, for all his talk of gnomic resonance, is to remove its ambiguity by a route opposite to the one taken by the French translator. Despite changes of emphasis and implication from one of his versions to the next, he has replied to a possible range of senses with another, mutually confirming, range of his own. Freud's 'pre-Socratic' hesitation between alternative destinies for the psychical life has turned to imperturbable advocacy in Lacan's hands: one of those destinies is unfailingly better.

Where Freud's 'Wo Es war, soll Ich werden' comes and goes as a modulated refrain throughout Lacan's work, Poe's 'The Purloined Letter' achieves its prominence more directly: Lacan's extended discussion of the tale is placed at the start of *Écrits* as a ramifying fable of the analytic process and of the constitutive function of the signifier. In Poe's story an incriminating letter addressed to an 'illustrious personage' (a queen, we are to assume) is stolen by a machinating minister in the presence of the royal couple. The Queen sees everything, and the King nothing. The Queen remains silent as the robbery takes place: to protest would be to incriminate herself. The Prefect of Police is given the task of recovering the letter and, having failed, consults the detective Dupin. The police are well-meaning plodders and the detective is all-seeingly astute. Whereas the police search the minister's apartment inch by inch and find nothing, Dupin, who knows his man and reasons that the safest form of concealment would be to leave the letter in full view of the visitor, finds the letter and steals it back. The contents of the letter are never revealed.

Part of the appeal which the story holds for Lacan will be apparent even from this simplistic summary. The purloined letter is a pure migratory signifier. As it passes from hand to hand, and moves from point to point within a complex web of intersubjective perception (Poe speaks of the 'robber's knowledge of the loser's knowledge of the robber'), it attracts different meanings to itself, mediates different kinds of power relationship and determines subjects in what they do and are:

Our fable is so constructed as to show that it is the letter and its diversion which governs their [the subjects'] entries and roles. If *it* be 'in sufferance' [*en souffrance*], *they* shall endure the pain. Should they pass beneath its shadow, they become its reflection. Falling in possession of the letter—admirable ambiguity of language—its meaning possesses them.

(Écrits)

Lacan's 'Le séminaire sur "La Lettre volée"' and its many associated documents, together with the earlier version published in *Séminaire* II, comprise an exegetical performance of rare subtlety. But is not Lacan's interpretation essentially an allegorical one? After all the mobile signifier, the *lettre volée* which is also a *feuille volante* ('flying page'), has been elicited by close reading and has become an immobile signified in the process: the mobility of the signifier is what Poe's story 'means', what it 'is about'. And is it not odd that allegory, which is meta-language *in excelsis*, should be written, and held to be illuminating, by one who holds meta-language to be impossible? Odd, yes; and inconsistent, and disappointing in the same way that Lacan's single-minded urging of sense upon Freud's 'Wo Es war . . .' is disappointing. But only if one confines one's attention to the broad, programmatic unfolding of Lacan's argument. If one looks at the fine structure of his writing, and the insistent play of ambiguity which permeates it, it becomes plain that even the basic psychoanalytic paradigms, and the habit of psychoanalytic explanation itself, may be called into question from within.

Lacan's practical debt to literature and the self-consciously 'writerly' status of his writing are apparent even to the casual reader. His admirers and his critics often give this writing, and especially the conspicuous presence within it of word-play, paradox, and counter-logical thinking, a prominent place in their arguments for, and against, the general validity of his work. Although an emphasis of this kind is in many ways misleading, and has led to serious misrepresentations of Lacan's achievement, there is no difficulty in seeing how 'mere' questions of style have achieved their unwonted importance within a theory of mind. For literature not only owns up more readily than other forms of language to its unconscious origins, but rejoices in the superabundance of sense to which it has access and in doing so offers the psychoanalyst a working model of the unconscious considered as an unstoppable and self-complicating signifying chain.

Poetry in particular is exemplary in this role:

But one has only to listen to poetry . . . for a polyphony to be heard, for it to become clear that all discourse is aligned along the several staves of a score.

There is in effect no signifying chain that does not have, as if attached to the punctuation of each of its units, a whole articulation of relevant contexts suspended "vertically", as it were, from that point.

(ibid.)

Lacan's theory seems to necessitate a certain kind of literary performance. If the unconscious is 'like poetry' in its overdetermined and polyphonic structures, then the writer who chooses to treat the unconscious, and wishes to obey its laws in his writing, must needs become more 'like a poet' the closer he gets to the quick of his subject. The overlapping and knotting together of signifiers within the written chain will show the reader what the unconscious is—and by enacting rather than describing it. Lacan here provides us with yet another pair of interdependent definitions. Poetry and the unconscious are mutually supporting: if you want to understand *a*, first understand *b*; if you want to understand *b*, first understand *a*. Yet on this occasion the entire conceptual construction is not free-floating but firmly planted in Lacan's glamorous and convoluted prose: this is the place where theories take on corporeal form and where Lacan's twin definitions prove themselves as *writing*.

Lacan's prose is an elaborate mechanism for multiplying and highlighting the connections between signifiers. Word-play abounds, and is given a great deal of intellectual work to do. Here are some examples with a brief comment on certain implications of each: 'la politique de l'autruiche': a policy which belongs at once to the ostrich (*autruche*), to others (*autrui*), and to Austria (*Autriche*, the birthplace of psychoanalysis); *'faufilosophe'*: a false (*faux*) philosopher (*philosophe*) who enters by stealth (*se faufile*); *'lettre–l'être–l'autre'*: the letter implies being implies the Other; *'dansité'*: density which dances; 'A casser l'œuf se fait l'Homme mais aussi *l'Hommelette'*: Man comes from the breaking of an egg, but so does the little man, the feminized man and the scrambled man; 'La loi en effet commanderait-elle: *Jouis*, que le sujet ne pourrait y répondre que par un *J'ouïs'*: when ordered to enjoyment, or to orgasm, the subject always answers 'I hear' (all the above from *Écrits*); *'poubellication'* (*Séminaire*, XX): to publish something is as good as throwing it in the dustbin (*poubelle*); '*âmour*' (ibid.): soul-love (*âme-amour*).

By these means language may be turned upon itself. Just as Joyce in *Finnegans Wake* creates 'tautaulogically' and in so doing makes the word 'tautologically' become what it describes, so Lacan, by writing '*la langue*' as '*lalangue*', inserts several facts of language into the name language bears: it is repetitious; it is an affair of the tongue (*langue*—our tongues beat our palates as we say it); it has a musical tendency (*la* is a note in the tonic sol-fa); it has a capacity to shock or surprise ('Oh là là!'). Wherever words collide and fuse in this way an atmosphere of play prevails. But an insistent doctrinal point may be heard in the background on each occasion: if the signifier plays and the signified 'slips beneath', then the unconscious is speaking in its native tongue.

Lacan speaks with approval of Humpty-Dumpty as 'the master of the signifier' and in his handling of portmanteau words proves himself a worthy heir of Carroll's aggressive talking egg. But he also speaks with approval of his own reputation as the 'Góngora' of psychoanalysis, and this second self-image—as the originator of a convoluted poetic style—is quite as revealing as the first. For Lacan has imagined a new pluralizing French syntax, as well as a new semantics. He savours the ambiguity of prepositions, for example, and plays relentlessly upon the alternative meanings of *à* and *de*. Earlier we saw him admiring the phrase 'en possession de' for meaning at once 'possessed by' and 'possessing'. A similar double meaning occurs in a sentence such as: 'le signifiant est unité d'être unique, n'étant de par sa nature symbole que d'une absence' (*Écrits*). The signifier is the symbol *of* an absence, and becomes a symbol *by means of* an absence. While in a preposition-laden passage like the following a rapid shimmer of alternative relationships will blur the vision of any reader seeking for a single main sense:

Man's freedom is entirely inscribed within the constituting triangle of the renunciation that he imposes on the desire of the other by the menace of death for the enjoyment of the fruits of his serfdom—of the consented-to sacrifice of his life for the reasons that give to human life its measure—and of the suicidal renunciation of the vanquished partner, depriving of his victory the master whom he abandons to his inhuman solitude.

(ibid.)

Each of these prepositions is a knot within the signifying chain; they are the moments of switch-over from one possible relationship to another—moments at which condensation and displacement become palpable events.

A complete account of the characteristic features, syntactic and other, of Lacan's style would include: the ambiguous *que*, disturbances of conventional word order, literal and metaphorical senses interwoven, periphrasis, ellipsis, leading notions alluded to rather than declared, abstractions personified, persons becoming abstractions, widely different words becoming synonyms, synonyms being given widely different meanings. . . . All this keeps the signified as a palely fluttering presence behind the rampaging signifier.

It is plain that a writer who uses these devices so frequently and in such close conjunction is not merely running the risk of writing nonsense, but is envisaging nonsense as a positive literary goal. For Lacan irony and contradiction are inherent in language, and psychology, in so far as it studies discourse, is 'the realm of the senseless'. When Lacan's 'truth'—the truth of the unconscious—is personified and allowed to talk in its own voice, as in the lecture called 'La Chose freudienne', it makes this point:

I wander about in what you regard as being the least true in essence: in the dream, in the way the most far-fetched conceit [*la pointe la plus gongorique*], the most grotesque nonsense of the joke [*calembour*] defies sense, in chance, not in its law, but in its contingence, and I never do more to change the face of the world than when I give it the profile of Cleopatra's nose.

(ibid.)

Lacan was decisively influenced by Surrealism in the late 1920s and early '30s: he had members of the group among his friends; he contributed articles on paranoia to the review *Minotaure*; he was impressed by the Surrealists' experiments in automatic writing and confirmed by Crevel, Éluard, and Joë Bousquet in his view that the writings of 'Aimée', the patient whose case history formed the basis for his doctoral research on paranoia, showed remarkable poetic power. *Écrits* contains countless references and allusions to the movement. There is little doubt that the newcomer to Lacan who already has some experience of Surrealist writing will hear many familiar notes being sounded in his work; and such a reader will be well equipped to understand how it is that nonsense may be thought of as a plenitude rather than an absence of sense and given a special role in exploring and proclaiming the truths of the unconscious.

But the young Lacan learned many lessons other than those of the Surrealists, and in later years wooed the unconscious with wiles and artifices far subtler than theirs. 'Nonsense' appears in the Lacan text now as a heady atmosphere of meanings promised but not given, now as an outrageous intruder into the world of rational argument or oratorical persuasion: the 'Cleopatra's nose' episode at the end of the passage I have just quoted is clearly of this second kind. But in both cases nonsense is an agent of intellectual provocation rather than a static display of psychical structure or a route towards the Surrealist *merveilleux*. It is a reminder to his own discourse that its responsibility is to 'dire toujours Autre-chose' (say always an Other-thing). For in Lacan's view the person who speaks and is satisfied with what he says is not simply misguided: he is wrong. Every statement that does not provoke change and strangeness within itself is wrong. Truth which seeks to remove itself from the contradictory process of language becomes falsehood there and then.

How puzzling it is, on first reading this self-proclaiming Freudian loyalist, to find that his works apparently resemble those of the master in no single particular of style, presentation, or intellectual convention. Where Freud is respected, even by those who reject his ideas or would wish to qualify them severely, as being patient and clear-headed in his expositions, able to give due weight to views other than his own in putting his arguments together, and scrupulous in specifying those areas of thought to which his theory is at present or permanently incapable of contributing, Lacan is irascible, peremptory, scornful of contrary opinions, by turns rhapsodic and assertive in his prose style, and plainly unconvinced that his theory anywhere has limits. Lacan does things in a way so different from Freud's that his enterprise can easily be seen, at first encounter, as an act of publicity-seeking sabotage directed at the very foundations of psychoanalysis.

His difference from Freud, and especially the high buffoonery which marks much of his writing, is dwelt on with glee in the many hostile responses to which his thought gives rise. Most published responses of this kind are trivial and written by self-righteous bystanders who have tried and failed, or simply failed, to read what Lacan writes. But his detractors are not all of this order and charges of, say, obscurantism made against him by intelligent and responsible authors cannot be ignored.

Sebastiano Timpanaro, for example, whose *The Freudian Slip* (1974) is a brilliant critique of *The Psychopathology of Everyday Life* conducted from the combined viewpoints of Marxism and textual criticism, writes in that work:

I must confess that I am incurably committed to the view that in Lacan's writings charlatanry and exhibitionism largely prevail over any ideas of a comprehensible, even if debatable, nature: behind the smoke-screen, it seems to me, there is nothing of substance; and it is difficult to think of a pioneer in the encounter between psychoanalysis and linguistics who has more frequently demonstrated such an erroneous and confused knowledge of the latter, whether structural or not.

Timpanaro's remarks show signs of a limited knowledge of Lacan and premature judgement. But the fact that such remarks are possible from one who in other matters knows much and judges well will clearly make us ask whether they might represent the polemical surface of a substantial case against Lacan. It is possible, after all, that critics of Timpanaro's kind, having informed themselves fully, would wish to leave the thrust of their judgement undiminished.

Let me mention some of the simplest and least specialized factors which an informed critique of Lacan might concentrate on. Lacan has taken extreme precautions to prevent his work from being made banal and comfortable in the wake of Freud's, and this striving to impede the facile re-transmission of his ideas often appears as a calculated effort to be unreadable. Just as you can gain access to the cave of the unconscious only by being inside already, he seems to be saying, so you can gradually reach towards an understanding of my work only by understanding it in advance. Lacan offers us a new conception both of science and of truth, and asks us to abandon many of the procedures for verification or falsification on which the credibility of scientific enquiry traditionally rests. Truth-to-the-unconscious is the only truth worth the

name. The desiring unconscious, and language which is its structure, are plural, layered, involuted, uncodifiable and unstoppable;
arguments directed towards a terminus are falsehoods.

But the paradox in all this is precisely that *all* language is the
metonymic displacement of desire; there is no meta-language, as
Lacan repeatedly insists, no Other for the Other, no truth about
truth. Why then is a sumptuously polyvalent language to be
preferred to the one-thing-at-a-time languages of logic, or conceptual analysis, or empirical description, or traditional psychoanalytic theory? Is it simply that such a language, having more goals for
desire visibly on the move within it, may be thought to maintain a
closer, more robust contact with the matrix of desire? But that
matrix is everywhere and inescapable. We saw Lacan himself
pointing to a version of the same paradox in his discussion of 'Wo
Es war, soll Ich werden': by what right, and with what moral goal
in view, can one urge man to become what he necessarily and
unfailingly is? Why set in motion such an elaborate machinery of
persuasion when there is strictly no one to persuade? As we read
Lacan, we can feel his arguments being traversed by weighty and
unargued personal predilections.

A related set of questions is raised by his expository manner. His
theory disallows any distinction between descriptive and prescrip-
tive writing, or between the practical analysis of cases and the
working out of relevant theoretical perspectives. He relies greatly
on the convincingness of certain recurrent maxims enshrining
crucial points of doctrine. These gnomic formulae are often
launched, repeated, and modulated without supporting argument.
They may be set as sudden pockets of relative clarity within a
mystifying tangle of word-games and poetic images; they may
appear side by side with vituperative assaults on the alleged falsi-
fiers of psychoanalytic thought. (For Lacan all issues are issues of
principle, and all local disagreements reveal the forces of darkness
and light in mighty combat.) Argumentative support does of
course converge on these sentences from elsewhere, and the reader
who is able to think in several directions at once will be at a distinct
advantage in fitting these materials together. But a writer's
prophecies may be all too neatly self-fulfilling when his ideas are
presented to us in this form.

One might parody the procedure thus: 'If what I say—about

language, the unconscious, the Other, the displacement of desire—were true, one would expect writing of a certain kind to be called forth; my writing exists and is of the expected kind; therefore what I say is true.' Or again: 'Ellipsis is a characteristic mode of unconscious mental functioning; so that if I omit main pieces of evidence in stating my case the rules of the unconscious are being obeyed and the truth is being told.' Circularity and question-begging never appear quite as nakedly as this in Lacan's thinking, but they are the risks that it unashamedly runs. He constantly subjects his thought to tests of his own devising; and his thought invariably passes them. Although many notable conceptual systems are invoked as he proceeds—those of Plato, Hegel, and Heidegger, for example—these do not provide any manner of external test for his own system. On the contrary, they provide that system with further dialectical challenge, further Otherness—which means, of course, further impetus and support. As contradiction is inherent in language, and as all language thereby becomes, in some sense, self-critical, no external tests are necessary. And to fail a test is, in any case, also to pass it.

This fantasy of omnipotence does not make Lacan's central contributions to psychoanalysis any the less impressive, although it may at first make them difficult for many readers to isolate. The fact that his published work has a pronounced air of narcissistic ostentation has helped it to acquire its improbable prestige within contemporary French culture. In buying *Écrits* you buy an event and a badge. And as the slogans of *Écrits* are part of the tittle-tattle of a capital city, you have no need to read a word of it in order to appropriate its magic. Future sociologists of knowledge will no doubt study the mechanisms whereby an enfeebled 'Lacanism', resembling the *'fofreudisme'* which Lacan caricatures, has come to loom larger within the intellectual life of a society than the original ideas and texts.

But in the meantime it is clear that Lacan's ideas, when situated and evaluated within their proper context, are strong enough to survive the false apotheosis to which fashionable opinion has elevated them. For it is in the psychoanalytic context, which is a practical and collaborative one, that they have already been put to work and severely tested. Independent-minded followers such as the French psychoanalytical writers Jean Laplanche, J.-B. Pontalis, Serge Leclaire, and Octave Mannoni are extending and refashioning Lacan's concepts without attempting to imitate his literary manner. It is plain from their work that Lacan is the originator of a coherent and continuing tradition of scientific enquiry.

Lacan has made Freud properly readable for the first time in France. His attention to facts of language as they appear in Freud's thinking, and to the ways in which structural linguistics may be used to reorganize the psychoanalytic account of the unconscious, have had numerous practical and theoretical repercussions within the French centres of the movement. I shall mention two of the most far-reaching of these. First, psychoanalysis has been recalled to an awareness of its intellectual responsibilities:

> Psychoanalysis will provide a scientific basis for its theory or for its technique only by formalizing in an adequate fashion the essential dimensions of its experience which, together with the historical theory of the symbol, are: intersubjective logic and the temporality of the subject.
>
> (*Écrits*)

An ambition of this kind sets Lacan apart from such well-known psychiatric radicals as R. D. Laing, David Cooper, and Thomas Szasz. For these writers *ideas* have a limited warrant: they are of use chiefly as a means of exposing the faulty premises on which repressive notions of sanity and madness are based, but contribute weakly if at all to descriptive or analytic accounts of psychical process. For Lacan, on the other hand, the exposure of faulty premises is merely part of a continuous process of psychical model-building in which ideas, gathered from a variety of sources, play a vital role. The attempt to formalize such hazardous areas of enquiry as 'intersubjective logic' and the 'temporality of the subject' is still at a primitive stage. What Lacan has done, drawing primarily on linguistics but also upon formal logic and mathematics, is to suggest ways in which intellectual rigour might become possible in branches of psychology where vagueness and guesswork have reigned until now.

Secondly, in drawing attention to the central importance of linguistic mediation within the human subject and within the analytic dialogue, Lacan has reformulated the goals of psychoanalysis both as a therapeutic method and as a moral discourse: 'Analysis can have for its goal only the advent of a true speech [*une parole vraie*] and the realization by the subject of his history in his relation to a future' (ibid.). The 'true speech' which analysis seeks to foster is one in which the subject is brought into full contact with that primary language of desire which is over-heard in his accounts of his dreams and symptoms. But this speech is possible only when the subject is able to acknowledge the plain facts of lack and incompleteness within himself. It is upon these facts that the Symbolic order is founded, and to inhabit that order is to accept that one's destiny as a subject is one of indefinite displacement.

The Imaginary alternative is seductive, and seems to promise an entire spectrum of fulfilments: identity, integrity, harmony, tranquillity, maturity, selfhood.... At moments Lacan treats the Imaginary and its concomitant array of worthy-seeming goals with a dismissive shrug: 'Seek these things if you wish, and if you're prepared to settle for baubles and lies; *truth*, of course, is elsewhere.' But in general his handling of the relations between the Symbolic and the Imaginary is at a much higher level of seriousness and complexity. Indeed his account of the unceasing dialectic between them which is ingrained in human living has given back to psychoanalysis much of the sombre moral resonance to be found in Freud's *Beyond the Pleasure Principle, Civilization and its Discontents*, and his late essay on 'Analysis Terminable and Interminable' Lacan's tone even here is quite unlike Freud's, but his refusal to surrender himself to the comforts of optimism or pessimism, and his steadfastness in the face of the irremediable, are of the same high order.

Lacan is widely influential outside psychoanalysis. One of the main reasons for this is that his writing proposes itself consciously as a critique of all discourses and all ideologies. He provides workers in other fields with a cautionary portrait of thinking-as-it-happens, and of the elements of Utopianism and infantile fantasy which may find their way even into the most austere and lucid operations of mind. 'Builders of conceptual monuments, beware!' is the message of *Écrits* to those who would hear.

For Lacan, Freud's revolution was 'ungraspable but radical'. And his own has been of the same kind. As he exposes the forces of repression operating within psychoanalytic systems and institutions, and allows the repressed to return in his own writing, he sets before us an extraordinarily original view of what thinking might be. He is a reader of Freud. But his fidelity to Freud is of a different kind from that of Plotinus to Plato or Maimonides to Aristotle. Freud provides him with a guarantee that all thinking is 'thinking other': there is no stability, no stopping place, no supreme system. The speaking unconscious is a model for the intellectual life. Rather than create a monument and leave time, history, or opinion to bring it down, Lacan writes works which displace and deconstruct themselves as they are produced. The thinking he shows us is one which inhabits time, proclaims itself as process, and finds its truth in its incompleteness.

Bibliography

Jacques Lacan was born in Paris in 1901, and received his medical training in the Paris Medical Faculty, where he became Chef de Clinique in 1932. He entered the psychoanalytical movement in 1936. In 1959 he was expelled from the International Psychoanalytical Association, and in 1964 founded the École Freudienne in Paris. He is now president of the 'Champ Freudien' department of the University of Vincennes.

BOOKS
Écrits (Paris, 1966); English translation, *Écrits: A Selection* (London and New York, 1977)

Le Séminaire
    Livre I: *Les Écrits techniques de Freud* (Paris, 1975)
    Livre II: *Le Moi dans la théorie de Freud et dans la technique de la psychanalyse* (Paris, 1978)
    Livre XI: *Les Quatre Concepts fondamentaux de la psychanalyse* (Paris, 1973); English translation, *The Four Fundamental Concepts of Psychoanalysis* (London, 1977; New York, 1978)
    Livre XX: *Encore* (Paris, 1975)

De la psychose paranoïaque dans ses rapports avec la personnalité (Paris, 1932); reprinted with *Premiers Écrits sur la paranoïa* (Paris, 1975)

Télévision (Paris, 1974)

Valuable background reading is J. Laplanche and J.-B. Pontalis, *The Language of Psychoanalysis* (London, 1973). Two volumes of *Yale French Studies*, nos. 48 (1972) and 55/6 (1977), entitled respectively 'French

Freud' and 'Literature and Psychoanalysis', are also helpful. *The Language of the Self* (Baltimore, Md., 1968) is an annotated translation by Anthony Wilden of Lacan's essay 'Fonction et champ de la parole et du langage en psychanalyse'.

Jacques Derrida

JONATHAN CULLER

Although the work of Jacques Derrida is a major force in contemporary literary and philosophical debate, it is too early to predict what will prove to have been his most powerful contribution. When we look back in twenty, in fifty, in a hundred years, will he prove to have inaugurated a new era in the history of philosophy? Will he have been responsible for a new mode of reading and interpretation and an accompanying theory of the nature of texts? Will he be seen as a key figure in the development and reorientation of an intellectual movement which will doubtless by then have a new name but which will encompass what we now think of as structuralism and post-structuralism? Rather than venture predictions about the significance future developments will give to his work, the best strategy is to approach his writings from several perspectives, creating, from the texts that bear his name, three Derridas, three projects which are important for us today.

First, as a philosopher, as a reader of philosophical texts, Derrida has demonstrated the persistence in the Western philosophical tradition of what he calls 'logocentrism' or the 'metaphysics of presence'. He argues that the different theories and theses of philosophy are versions of a single system, and though we cannot hope to escape this system we can at least identify the conditions of thought it imposes by attending to that which it seeks to repress. Though we cannot imagine or bring about the *end* of metaphysics, we can undertake a critique of it from within by identifying and reversing the hierarchies it has established. In his dealings with philosophical texts, Derrida has produced a powerful and critical account of Western thought.

Secondly, Derrida is a reader, an interpreter. His readings of a variety of texts—Rousseau, Saussure, Freud, Plato, Genet, Hegel, Mallarmé, Husserl, J. L. Austin, Kant—have become, for those alert to the adventures of intelligence, exemplary analyses, models

154

of a new practice of interpretation. Attentive to the ways in which texts implicitly criticize and undermine the philosophies in which they are implicated, he carries on a double mode of reading, showing the text to be woven from different strands which can never result in a synthesis but continually displace one another. This new practice of reading and writing is making itself felt particularly in the realm of literary criticism.

Finally, from the point of view of this volume, Derrida is one of a group of innovative French thinkers, who can be loosely labelled 'structuralist and post-structuralist' and whose efforts in a variety of disciplines have created if not a movement (for they would certainly wish to stress their disagreements with one another), at least a force. The work of each has focused on problems of language and structure and the cumulative effect, even of their disagreements, has been a powerful impetus to a certain style of thought and set of concerns. But precisely because structuralism and its aftermath constitute not a unified theory but a complex network of writings interacting in various ways, it is extremely difficult to map and to interpret them. Derrida's special importance lies in the fact that he alone, among the five thinkers whom this volume has singled out, has written about the works of the others, relating them to central problems of structuralist and post-structuralist theory, and thus providing a perspective which helps us to understand what is at stake in the intellectual enterprises to which the present book refers.

Each of these contributions by Derrida is, of course, a major enterprise, and to attribute all three of them to a single writer must seem to be casting him in the role of supreme master of theory and textuality: author of a comprehensive theory which can place and account for other theories and explicate the works in which they are expressed. Certainly for most people who have become familiar with Derrida's work, this is the effect it has: an effect of mastery. But both Derrida and his admirers repeatedly stress that he does not propose a comprehensive or unified theory that would master and explain literature, language, philosophy. Derrida always writes about particular texts, and the kind of writing which he practises and would like to inspire in others explores precisely the impossibility of such comprehensive mastery, the impossibility of constructing a coherent and adequate theoretical system. Unlike most theorists, who build a system around several key concepts, Derrida is continually giving strategic roles to new terms, usually taken from the texts he is discussing; and these terms acquire a special salience from the structural complexity of the role they play in the interaction of Derrida's text with that other text. Derrida continually introduces new terms, displacing the old, in order to prevent any of them from becoming the central concepts of a new theory or system.

But of course he can never prevent this from happening. As his work is read and discussed, as it takes effect, it will inevitably be treated as a theory with central concepts, with analytical methods, making general claims about the nature of language and texts. Even if one grants that it is his dealings with texts rather than any explicit theory which ought to be stressed, as soon as one cites or presents these readings they become examples of analytical practice and thus illustrations of a theory and method. The very nature of intellectual discussion, as Derrida himself would be only too quick to point out, involves effects of mastery and hence the formulation of general claims, such as can be inferred from his practice of reading and writing. Even to say, as I have done, that Derrida's readings are attentive to everything in language and textuality which resists and exceeds general summary, is to produce just such a formulation.

We find ourselves, then, in a paradoxical situation, and doubtless many readers are inclined to dismiss any such line of thought —on the assumption that there must be perfectly good non-paradoxical solutions to any problem. But there is much we can learn from Derrida provided we do not close our minds in advance to the possibility which so much of his work explores: that the exercise of language and thought involves us in intractable paradoxes, which we can not escape but only repress. A good first step might be that very combination of exasperation and insight which we feel when we grasp that any attempt to give an account of what Derrida says is a falsification of his project, but that such falsification is unavoidable: it is unavoidable because even to identify it is to commit the error—the necessary error—one is identifying.

The best strategy for approaching Derrida's work, then, may be a double one: since even the most subtle and scrupulous formulations would not avoid the problem of 'misrepresentation', I shall, on the one hand, present general theoretical claims without apology; yet, on the other hand, in order to counteract the impression that will be given by these discussions of general theory, I will follow portions of Derrida's interpretive arguments in some detail so that the reader will gain some sense of his way with texts. Before undertaking this double exposition, however, it may be useful to provide, by way of introduction, a brief listing of Derrida's works and the major preoccupations of each.

Derrida was trained in philosophy, the subject which he now teaches at the École Normale Supérieure in Paris. His first work, *L'Origine de la géometrie*, was published in 1962 and consists of a 170-page introduction to a paper by the German philosopher Edmund Husserl on the origin of geometry. Husserl was interested in the relationship between the ideal objectivity of geometry (the 'laws' of geometry do not depend on any historical or empirical event) and its empirical historical existence (particular individuals propose geometric laws or proofs). To the question how geometry as a thought in the mind of a geometer can become geometry as ideal object, Husserl answers that language and in particular writing, with its impersonality, is the condition of this possibility. Derrida's subtle analysis of the strategies and presuppositions of Husserl's argument shows that though language is being offered as a solution, it contains within itself the problems it is supposed to solve. These problems, of the relation between event and structure, the empirical and the ideal, system and origin, and speech and writing have become the subject of most of Derrida's later work.

L'Origine de la géometrie won a philosophical prize but did not attract much attention outside the circle of philosophers concerned with Husserl and phenomenology. Shortly thereafter, however, Derrida began publishing essays in French intellectual periodicals, and in 1967 he suddenly imposed himself on the intellectual scene with three books, *Of Grammatology, Writing and Difference,* and *Speech and Phenomena*.

Of Grammatology is perhaps Derrida's best-known work. It concerns the way in which those who write about language have always privileged speech over writing and about what is at stake in that hierarchization. Arguing that all those qualities which are said to characterize writing, as distinct from speech, turn out to hold for speech also, Derrida considers the possibility, alluded to in his title (grammatology = the science of writing), of inverting the hierarchy and orienting a theory of language not on speech but on a generalized writing. The principal authors discussed in this book are Ferdinand de Saussure, the founder of modern linguistics, and Jean-Jacques Rousseau, one of whose many works is an 'Essay on the Origin of Language'; I will consider Derrida's reading of Saussure in some detail below.

Writing and Difference is a collection of essays on the works of major contemporary figures and the general theoretical tendencies they represent: Jean Rousset and structuralist literary criticism, Michel Foucault, Edmond Jabès, Emmanuel Levinas, Husserl, Antonin Artaud, Freud, Georges Bataille, Claude Lévi-Strauss and structuralism in the human sciences. By the accidents of publication this last essay on Lévi-Strauss, written for a conference at The Johns Hopkins University in 1966 and translated into English for the proceedings of that conference, was for a time the work by which Derrida was principally known in the English-speaking world. Analysing certain problems in Lévi-Strauss's method, Derrida concludes by contrasting two views of interpretation—one retrospective, which attempts to reconstruct an original meaning or truth, the other prospective, which explicitly welcomes the indeterminacy of meaning—and though he says that we are not able to choose between these alternatives, he was widely understood as opting for the second and was thus viewed as an apostle of 'free play'. In addition to this essay, which had a historical importance inasmuch as it created a certain image of Derrida, the chapter on Freud and the models involving writing which are used to represent the psyche, is an essential discussion for recent theory.

Speech and Phenomena, unlike the other two books of 1967, is a unified work of philosophical analysis concerned with Husserl's theory of signs and in particular with the role and status in phenomenology of the notions of voice and presence. Husserl's account views signs as derivative and dependent indications of meaning, which, in turn, is seen as what is present to consciousness at the moment of utterance. Derrida shows that by Husserl's own account of time, meaning can never be, as he wished, a simple presence, something given in and of itself, but is always part of a system of 'traces' and contrasts which exceeds any present instant. Derrida's analysis is what we now call a 'deconstruction' of Husserl's text: a demonstration that the logic of Husserl's argument 'undoes' itself and thus involves a central paradox or self-contradiction which is a basic insight into the matter under discussion. The themes explicitly treated in this lucid and scrupulous book will emerge repeatedly in my discussion of Derrida's other analyses and his general enterprise.

These three books made Derrida into a major figure in the theoretical debates which dominated French intellectual life in the late 1960s. Though associated with structuralism by his opponents, Derrida repeatedly produced readings which demonstrated the paradoxes of structuralist positions. In 1972 he once again brought out three books composed of such readings and other material: *Marges de la philosophie*, *La Dissémination*, and *Positions*.

Marges de la philosophie is a collection of ten essays: 'La Différance', an important text which I shall discuss later; *'Ousia* et *grammè'*, on Heidegger's discussion of the metaphysics of presence; 'Le Puits et la pyramide', on Hegel's theory of the sign; 'Les Fins de l'homme', on the status of humanism in the light of Heidegger's writings; 'Le Cercle linguistique de Genève', on Rousseau, Condillac, and Saussure; 'La Forme et le vouloir dire', on Husserl's phenomenology of language; 'Le Supplément de copule', on linguistic and philosophical problems of the verb 'to be'; 'La Mythologie blanche', an important essay on metaphor and philosophy; 'Qual quelle', on the notion of 'source', with reference to Paul Valéry and to Freud; and 'Signature, événement, contexte', on J. L. Austin and the problem of speech acts. This is a book of subtle philosophic argument.

La Dissémination, which contains three 100-page essays and a long preface, is more oblique and 'literary'. It is concerned precisely with the literary, in so far as the 'literary' is our name for effects of language which escape conceptual determination and are not reducible to a concept. The preface discusses the problem of prefaces which, by saying what a book says before it says it, are supposed to give a unity to the volume of which they are both a part and not a part (the volume which includes them and the text which they precede). The first essay, 'La Pharmacie de Platon', is a study of the notion of writing in Plato and of the term *pharmakon*, which—both 'poison' and 'remedy'—plays a strategic role in the logic of Plato's text. 'La Double Séance' takes a brief text of Mallarmé's as its point of departure for a discussion of mimesis (representation, imitation) and its intractable paradoxes. The final essay, 'La Dissémination', works with an experimental novel by Philippe Sollers, *Nombres*, to provide both an account and an example of 'dissémination': a linguistic or textual productivity which escapes the domination of or determination by concepts. Whereas the notion of ambiguity assumes the possibility of enumerating and thus controlling meanings, dissemination is a semantic dispersal, produced by various effects of order or resemblance, which can never be completely controlled. *La Dissémination*, in its exploration of these problems, is Derrida's most forbidding and difficult book.

Positions, on the other hand, which contains the texts of three interviews, is extremely lucid and doubtless the best introduction to Derrida that there is. The first interview, 'Implications', is a general commentary on his work up until 1967. The second, 'Sémiologie et grammatologie', is a succinct discussion of the theory of the sign and Derrida's critique of it. The last, 'Positions', contains an account of 'deconstruction' and remarks on numerous other subjects, including history, Marxism, and Jacques Lacan.

In 1974 Derrida published *Glas*, a book which has become notorious for its presentation if not for its argument. On the left-hand column of each page Derrida conducts an analysis of the concept of the family in Hegel (including paternal authority, Absolute knowledge, the Holy Family, and the Immaculate Conception). In the right-hand column, facing the author of *The Philosophy of Right*, is the thief and homosexual, Jean Genet. Citations from and discussions of the works of Genet are woven together with remarks on the double bind and the problem of the signature, and a punning exploration of words linked by phonetic resemblances and etymological chains. Constantly at work in the text is the problematical relationship between the two columns: always offered as a possibility but never affirmed and never, except by a wilful act on the part of the reader, giving rise to a synthesis.

In addition to these books, there are numerous uncollected articles, especially from the period since *Glas*, which ought to be mentioned. 'Où commence et comment finit un corps enseignant?'

and 'L'Âge de Hegel' bear on the teaching of philosophy and its institutional framework. 'Le Facteur de la vérité' is an important analysis of Lacan. 'Éperons', on Nietzsche, style, the idea of woman, and the conditions of interpretation, has appeared as a separate volume with versions in four languages. 'Economimesis' is a powerful deconstruction of Kantian and Romantic aesthetic theory, and, along with 'Le Parergon'[1]—on the relationship between the frame and what it frames—constitutes a major theoretical advance. There are, in addition, papers on Maurice Blanchot, Francis Ponge, and Condillac which all have their points of interest. A reader who knows French should begin with *Positions* and then turn to texts whose ostensible subjects already interest him. One whose explorations are confined to translations might start with Part Two of *Of Grammatology*, unless a familiarity with philosophy enables him to begin with the more ordinary exposition and argument of *Speech and Phenomena*.

What is the nature of the project to which all these writings contribute? Derrida's readings of various texts and the constructions of his own texts are explorations of Western 'logocentrism'. The 'metaphysics of presence', which these texts can be shown simultaneously to affirm and to undermine, is the only metaphysics we know and underlies all our thinking; but it can be shown to give rise to paradoxes that challenge its coherence and consistency and therefore challenge the possibility of determining or defining being as presence. The framework of the history of metaphysics, Derrida writes,

is the determination of being as *presence* in all the senses of this word. It would be possible to show that all the terms related to fundamentals, to principles, or to the centre have always designated the constant of a presence—*eidos, archè, telos, energeia, ousia* (essence, existence, substance, subject), *aletheia*, transcendentality, consciousness or conscience, God, man, and so forth.

(Writing and Difference)

Three examples will help to illustrate what is involved in the metaphysics of presence. In the Cartesian *cogito*, 'I think, therefore I am', the *I* is deemed to lie beyond doubt because it is present to

[1]Now collected, with other essays on art, in *La Vérité en peinture* (1978).

itself in the act of thinking. The proposition 'I am, I exist' is necessarily true, Descartes says, 'each time I pronounce it or conceive it in my mind'. Or consider, as a second example, our familiar notion that the present instant is what exists. The future will exist and the past did exist but the reality of each depends on its relation to the presence of a present: the future is an anticipated presence and the past a former presence. A third instance would be the notion of meaning (when we speak to each other) as something present to the consciousness of the speaker, which is then expressed through signs or signals: meaning is what the speaker 'has in mind' at the crucial moment.

As these three examples indicate, the metaphysics of presence is pervasive and familiar. What is perhaps less obvious is the way in which the nature and reality of things in the universe, including numerous things which transcend any given instant, is thought to be grounded on this kind of presence. Thus, Descartes argues for the existence of the self (which we usually think of as the relatively permanent core of an individual) by claiming that at each instant of consciousness there is necessarily something (an I) which is conscious. Or again, the reality of a tree is made to depend on the fact that there is a tree there at time x, at time y, and again at time z; its existence is a series of presences. Finally, when we say that a given word means such and such, we can argue that this is a form of shorthand for the fact that at time x someone used the word to signify such and such, which was the concept present in his mind; at time y someone else used the word in the same sense, and so on.

Reality is thus made up of a series of present states. These states are what is basic, the elementary constituents which are given and on which our account of the universe depends. This view is powerful and persuasive, but there is a problem which it characteristically encounters. When we invoke these states or moments of presence which are supposedly so basic, we discover that they are themselves already dependent in various ways and therefore cannot serve as the simple givens on which explanation must rest.

Consider, for example, the flight of an arrow. If we focus on a series of present states we encounter a paradox: at any given time the arrow is at a particular spot; it is always in a particular spot and never in motion. Yet we want to insist, quite justifiably, that the arrow *is* in motion at every instant between the beginning and the end of its flight. When we focus on present states, the motion of the arrow is never present, never given. It turns out that motion, which is after all a fundamental reality of our world, is only conceivable in so far as every instant, every present state, is already marked with the traces of the past and the future. An account of what is happening at a given instant requires reference to other instants which are not present. There is thus a crucial sense in which the non-present inhabits and is part of the present. The motion of the arrow is never given as something simple and present which could be grasped in itself; it is always already complex and differential, involving traces of the *not-now* in the *now*.

This is one of the Greek philosopher Zeno's famous paradoxes. Others, less dramatic but no less intractable, arise in whatever domain one investigates. Generally, one can say, with Derrida, that nothing is ever simply present. Anything that is supposedly present and given as such is dependent for its identity on differences and relations which can never be present. But the fact that differences are not present doesn't mean that they are absent. Our language is so suffused with the metaphysics of presence that it seems to offer us only this alternative: either something is present or else it is absent. The Derridean critique of this metaphysics involves, among other things, identifying elements, terms, and functions which, like 'difference', are difficult to conceive within this framework and which, when brought to the fore, work not so much to discredit that framework as to indicate its limits. Difference resists discussion in terms of the opposition presence/absence.

This will perhaps become clearer if we consider a second example of the paradoxes that arise within this system of thinking. This one bears on signification and might be called the paradox (or *aporia*) of structure and event. We tend to think that what we call the meaning of a word depends on the fact that it has been used by speakers on various occasions with the intention of communicating or expressing this meaning, and we thus might want to argue that what can in general be called the structure of a language—the general system of its rules and regularities—is derived from and determined by events: by acts of communication. But if we took this argument seriously and began to look at the events which are said to determine structures, we would find that every event is itself already determined and made possible by prior structures. The possibility of meaning something by an utterance is already inscribed in the structure of the language. The structures, of course, are themselves always products, but however far back we try to push, even when we think about the birth of language itself and try to describe an originating event which might have produced the first structure, we discover that we must assume prior organization, prior differentiation. For a caveman successfully to originate language by making a special grunt signify something like 'food' is possible only if we assume that the grunt is already distinguished or distinguishable from other grunts and that the world has already been divided into the categories of food and non-food. Signification always depends on difference: contrasts, for example, between food and not-food which allow 'food' to be signified.

And when we think not about concepts but about the signifiers of a language, we find that the same applies. The sound sequence *pet*, for example, can function as a sign only because it contrasts with *bet*, *met*, *pat*, *pen*, etc. The noise one makes when one utters the sign *pet* is thus marked by the traces of these signs which one is not uttering. As we saw in the case of motion, what is present is itself complex and differential, marked by a series of differences. Derrida expands on this theme in *Positions*:

The play of differences involves syntheses and referrals [*renvois*] which prevent there from being at any moment or in any way a simple element which is *present* in and of itself and refers only to itself. Whether in written or spoken discourse, no element can function as a sign without relating to another element which itself is not simply present. This linkage means that each 'element'—phoneme or grapheme—is constituted with reference to the trace in it of the other elements of the sequence or system. Nothing, in either the elements or the system, is anywhere ever simply present or absent.

Signifying events depend on differences, but these differences are themselves the products of events. When one focuses on events one is led to affirm the priority of differences, but when one focuses on differences one sees their dependence on prior events. One can shift back and forth between these two perspectives which never give rise to a synthesis. Each perspective shows the error of the other in an irresolvable dialectic. This alternation Derrida terms *différance*. The French verb *différer* means both to differ and to defer. *Différance*, which did not previously exist in French, sounds exactly the same as *différence* (meaning 'difference'), but the ending in *a*, which is used elsewhere to produce noun forms from verbs, makes it a new form meaning 'a differing or a deferring'. *Différance* thus designates both a passive difference already in existence as the condition of signification and an act of differing or deferring which produces differences. A term that behaves similarly in English is *spacing*, which designates both a completed arrangement and an act of distribution or arranging. Derrida does on occasion use the corresponding French term *espacement*, but *différance* is more powerful and apposite precisely because *différence* is a key term in the writings of Nietzsche, Freud, and especially Saussure. Investigating systems of signification, those thinkers were led to stress differences and differentiation; and Derrida's silent deformation of *différence* by substituting an *a* for the *e* is a manœuvre which makes apparent the problematical complexity of signification by producing what, in our language, is not so much a concept as a contradiction.

Différance, he says,

is a structure and a movement which cannot be conceived on the basis of the opposition presence/absence. *Différance* is the systematic play of differences, of traces of differences, of the *spacing* [*espacement*] by which elements refer to one another. This spacing is the production, both active and passive (the *a* of *différance* indicates this indecision in relation to activity and passivity, indicates that which cannot be governed and organized by that opposition), of intervals without which the 'full' terms could not signify, could not function.

(*Positions*)

This preliminary account of the paradoxes of signification and the role of *différance* prepares us for further explorations of the theory of language in Derrida's reading of Saussure's *Course in General Linguistics* (trans. 1960). Saussure is generally regarded as the father of modern linguistics and his methodological distinctions have formed the basis for much structuralist theory, so a reading of his work can have important implications. Derrida finds in Saussure a powerful critique of the metaphysics of presence and what he calls its 'logocentrism', but also, and simultaneously, an unavoidable affirmation of this logocentrism and an inextricable involvement with it. I shall outline these two movements or moments in turn and then consider their significance.

Saussure begins by defining language as a system of signs—noises count as language only when they serve to express or communicate ideas—and thus the central question for him becomes the nature of the linguistic sign: what gives a sign its identity. He argues that signs are arbitrary and conventional and that each sign is defined not by some essential property but by the differences which distinguish it from other signs. The more rigorously he pursues his investigation, the more uncompromisingly he is led to argue that the sign is a purely relational unit and that 'in language there are only differences, *without positive terms*' (*Course in General Linguistics*). This is a principle wholly at odds with logocentrism and the metaphysics of presence. It maintains, on the one hand, that no terms of the system are ever simply and wholly present, for differences can never be present. And on the other hand it defines identity in terms of common absences rather than in terms of presence. Identity, which is the very cornerstone of any metaphysics, is made purely relational.

At the same time, however, there is in Saussure's argument a powerful affirmation of logocentrism. This emerges, most interestingly for Derrida, in Saussure's treatment of writing, which he relegates to a secondary, derivative status as compared with speaking. The object of linguistic analysis, Saussure writes, 'is not both the written and the spoken forms of words: the spoken forms alone constitute the object' (ibid.). Writing is simply a means of representing speech, a technical device, an external accessory, and need not therefore be taken into consideration when one is studying language.

This may seem a relatively innocent manœuvre, but in fact, as Derrida shows, it is crucial to the Western tradition of thinking about language, where speech is seen as natural, direct communication and writing as an oblique representation of a representation. Speaker and listener are present to one another and the words issue from the speaker as the spontaneous and nearly transparent signs of his present thought, which the listener can grasp. Writing, on the other hand, consists of physical marks which are divorced from the thought which may have led to their production; and it characteristically functions in the absence of either speaker or hearer. Writing gives uncertain access to the thought of the writer and it can even appear as wholly anonymous, unconnected with any speaker or author. It thus seems to be not merely a technical accessory for representing speech but more significantly a deformation or distortion of speech. This view of writing is as old as philosophy itself: in the *Phaedrus* Plato condemns writing as a bastardized form of communication; separated from the father or the moment of origin, writing can give rise to all sorts of misconceptions and misunderstandings, since the speaker is not there to explain to the listener what he has in mind.

Privileging speech in this way by treating writing as a parasitic and imperfect representation of it is a way of repressing or setting aside certain features of language, or certain aspects of its functioning. If distance, absence, misunderstanding, insincerity are features of writing, then by distinguishing writing from speech one can construct a model of communication which takes as the norm an ideal associated with speech—where the listener is thought to be able in principle to grasp precisely what the speaker has in mind. Indeed, the tone of moral fervour which marks Saussure's discussion of writing indicates that something important is at stake. He speaks of the 'dangers' of writing, which 'disguises' language and even on occasion 'usurps' the role of speech. The 'tyranny of writing' is powerful and insidious, leading, for example, to errors of pronunciation which are 'pathological', a corruption or infection of the natural spoken forms. Linguists who attend to written forms are 'falling into the trap'. Writing, supposedly an external accessory in the service of speech, threatens to taint the purity of the system it serves.

The relationship between speech and writing is therefore more complicated than it at first seemed. The hierarchical scheme that gave speech priority and made writing dependent on it has now been upset by the possibility that speech may not be independent of writing after all and that writing may affect and infect speech. The structure or play of relations at work here is one which Derrida has identified in a number of texts, particularly in Rousseau, and which he calls, using a term common in Rousseau, the 'logic of the *supplément*'. A supplement, *Webster's Dictionary* tells us, is 'something that completes or makes an addition'. When Rousseau says that education supplements nature, this produces a complicated concept of nature, for it is both something complete in itself, to which education is an addition, and something incomplete, or insufficient, which must be supplemented by education for it to be truly itself. In the latter case—and this is a respectable theory—education is needed in order to allow someone's true nature to emerge as what it is. The logic of supplementarity thus makes nature the prior term, a plenitude which was there at the start, but reveals an inherent lack or absence within it and makes education something external and extra but also an essential condition of that which it supplements.

Rousseau also speaks of masturbation as a 'dangerous supplement': like writing, it is a perverse addition—in this case to sexuality rather than to language—which does not affect the nature of normal sexuality. On the other hand, masturbation substitutes for, or takes the place of, normal sexual activity; its ability to act as substitute indicates that it may share something of the same nature; indeed it turns out that what characterizes masturbation—the focus on an imagined sexual object and the impossibility of possessing what one desires—is also true of normal sexual activity, whose moments are described in such a way that they become versions of a generalized masturbation.[2]

The logic of supplementarity, as Derrida describes it, is powerful and pervasive; it makes possible everything which we think of as human: language, passion, society, art. Once alerted to it, we can find it at work in the most diverse contexts. We are dealing with a logic of the supplement when something characterized as marginal with respect to a plenitude—as writing is marginal to the activity of speech or perversion to normal sexuality—is identified as a substitute for that plenitude or as something which can supplement or complete it. It then becomes possible to show that what were conceived as the distinguishing characteristics of the marginal are in fact the defining qualities of the central object of consideration. The supposed plenitude is inhabited from the outset by *différance*, which is both a division and deferral of plenitude.

---

[2] For these two examples see the chapter on 'The Dangerous Supplement' in *Of Grammatology*.

We shall see shortly how writing, that marginal supplement, proves to be the constitutive condition of language itself.

Saussure and others expend moral fervour in rejecting writing because they have identified it with certain characteristics of language which they want to set aside but which, precisely because they are characteristics of language, continually threaten to reappear. But one should not infer from Derrida's discussion that Saussure and his predecessors simply made a mistake in privileging speech over writing. This move is essential to our metaphysics:

> The privilege of the *phonè* does not depend upon a choice that could have been avoided. It responds to a moment of *economy* (let us say of the 'life' of 'history' or of 'being-as-self-relationship'). The system of 'hearing (understanding)-oneself-speak' [*s'entendre parler*] through the phonic substance—which presents itself as the non-exterior, non-mundane, therefore non-empirical or non-contingent signifier—has necessarily dominated the history of the world during an entire epoch, and has even produced the idea of the world, the idea of world-origin, that arises from the difference between the worldly and the non-worldly, the outside and the inside ideality and non-ideality, universal and non-universal, transcendental and empirical, etc.
>
> (*Of Grammatology*)

These are large claims. They may become more comprehensible if one notes that oppositions such as outside/inside, transcendental/empirical, worldly/non-worldly depend on a point of differentiation, a line of division where, for example, the inside is separated from the outside. It is only in relation to that point of differentiation, which controls the distinction between inside and outside, that the opposition can exist. Derrida's claim is that the moment of speaking, where signifier and signified or sound and meaning seem to be given together, where the inner and the outer, the material and the non-material, seem for a moment to be fused, serves as the point of reference in relation to which all these distinctions, which are essential to our metaphysics, can be posited. To tamper with the privilege of speech threatens the entire edifice.

The moment of speech can play this kind of role because it seems to be the one point or instant in which form and meaning are simultaneously present. Written words may be physical marks which a reader must interpret and animate, supplying meanings which he deems appropriate but which do not seem to be given in the words themselves. But when I speak, my words are not external material objects which I first hear and then interpret. At the moment of utterance my words seem to be transparent signifiers coextensive with my thought; at the moment of speech consciousness seems present to itself; concepts present themselves directly, as signifieds which my words will express for others. Voice seems to be the direct manifestation of thought and thus the meeting point of the physical and the intelligible, body and soul, empirical and transcendental, outside and inside, etc. This is what Derrida calls the system of *s'entendre parler*, of hearing and simultaneously understanding oneself speak: my words give me direct and immediate access to my thoughts, and this form of self-presence, this circuit of self-understanding, is taken as the model for communication in general—what true communication consists of when there are no external difficulties or forms of interference. Presence is the cornerstone of the theory of language and communication, and writing, defined in terms of presence, is seen as deficient or, at the very best, as an indirect restoration of a presence.

Voice is privileged so that language can be treated in terms of presence—a necessity if description or analysis is to get under way, since to identify signs one must be able to grasp meanings. But these posited presences, when one focuses on them, always turn out to be already inhabited by *différance*, or marked by absence. Saussure sets aside writing so as to deal with phonic units in their purity and simplicity, but writing returns at a crucial point: when he has to explain the nature of linguistic units. How can one explain that the units of a language have a purely differential nature? 'Since an identical state of affairs is observable in writing, another system of signs, we shall use writing to draw some comparisons that will clarify the whole issue' (*Course in General Linguistics*).[3] For example, the letter *t* can be written in various ways so long as it remains distinct from *l*, *f*, *i*, *d*, etc. There are no essential features which must be preserved; its identity is purely relational.

Thus writing, which Saussure claimed ought not to be the object of linguistic enquiry, turns out to be constructed on the very same principles as speech and to be the best illustration of the nature of linguistic units. There is at work here in Saussure's text an opera-

[3] See *Of Grammatology*, pp. 52–3.

tion of 'self-deconstruction', in which the text unmasks its own construction, reveals it as a rhetorical operation rather than a solid foundation. Having established a hierarchy that made writing a form derivative from speech, Saussure's own argument shows that this relationship can be reversed and presents speech as a species of writing, a manifestation of the principles that are at work in writing. Here the 'logic of the supplement' is displayed in the working of Saussure's own text. The marginal in its very marginality turns out to characterize the central object of discussion.

Pursuing this interplay of speech and writing in Saussure and other thinkers—Rousseau, Husserl, Lévi-Strauss, Condillac—Derrida produces a general demonstration that if writing is characterized by the qualities traditionally associated with it, then speech itself is already a form of writing. Not only, as Saussure says, do the units of speech have the relational character especially evident in writing, but precisely the kind of absence which was thought to distinguish writing from speech proves to be the condition of any sign at all. For any form to be a sign it must be repeatable—produceable or reproduceable—even in the absence of a communicative intention. It is part of the nature of every sign to be iterable, to be able to function cut off from any intended meaning, as if it were an anonymous mark. A cry, for example, is a sign only if it can be 'counterfeited', cited, or produced simply as an example. Since this possibility, which is one of the possibilities of writing as traditionally described, always attends the sign, the sign cannot be satisfactorily treated on the model of voice as self-presence. Reversing the hierarchy, we can treat speech as a species of writing, or rather, since the notion of writing must now be broadened to include speech, we might speak, as Derrida does, of an *archi-écriture*, an archi-writing or proto-writing, which is the condition of both speech and writing in the narrow sense.

It is precisely because language is a proto-writing, because presence is always both differed and deferred, that theorists have tried to relegate writing to a status of dependence. Derrida's deconstructive reversal suggests that instead of basing a theory on an idealized speech—in particular the circuit of hearing oneself speak, where meanings seem to be made immediately present by the spoken word—and treating actual utterances or texts as variously attenuated examples of this process, one might think of language as a play of differences, a proliferation of traces and repetitions which, under conditions that can be described but never exhaustively specified, give rise to effects of meaning.

But the perspective this offers is not an alternative discipline, a non-logocentric linguistics. 'This archi-writing', says Derrida,

> although its concept is *invoked* by the themes of the 'arbitrariness of the sign' and of difference, cannot and can never be recognized as the *object of a science*. It is that very thing which cannot let itself be reduced to the form of a presence. The latter orders all objectivity of the object and all relation of knowledge.
>
> (*Of Grammatology*)

The notions involved in the constitution of a discipline all derive from the system of presence in that at some point they subordinate the movement of *différance* to something autonomous and self-identical. 'Objectivity', for example, is a repeatable presence: the possibility of a repeated manifestation of self-identical objects or situations. The critique of logocentrism, in so far as it involves argument, demonstration, and appeals to evidence or notions of experience, is sustained by the very logocentrism which it seeks to breach. It remains within the system, revealing the *aporias* or contradictions which prevent it from being a fully coherent system. A new semiotics or science of meaning which would lie beyond logocentrism is an impossibility.

> One can say *a priori* that in every semiotic proposition or system of research metaphysical presuppositions will cohabit with critical motifs,[4] by virtue of the fact that up to a certain point they inhabit the same language, or rather the same system of language. Grammatology would doubtless be less another science, a new discipline charged with a new content or a new and clearly delimited domain, than the vigilant practice or exercise of this textual division [*la pratique vigilante de ce partage textuel*].
>
> (*Positions*)

Deconstruction thus undertakes a double reading, describing the ways in which lines of argument in the texts it is analysing call their premises into question, and using the system of concepts within which a text works to produce constructs, such as *différance* and *supplément*, which challenge the consistency of that system. But the fact that both Derrida's own texts and the texts he reads are based

---

[4] i.e. involving a critique of logocentrism.

on this 'cohabitation' of metaphysical presuppositions with critical motifs gives rise to a problem which does not so far seem to have been satisfactorily solved: how can we characterize the difference, if there is a difference, between what Derrida calls the 'textual division' in a grammatological text and the 'textual division' of other writings, or between the 'cohabitation' of motifs in Derrida's own writing and their cohabitation in the writings of the other contemporary theorists whom he criticizes?

The importance of this question becomes clear if we approach it from another angle. Deconstructive readings are often interpreted as attacks on the authors they discuss, since they reveal a self-contradiction or self-deconstruction and since we are accustomed to think that self-contradiction invalidates any intellectual enterprise. But if self-contradiction of a sort is, as Derrida tells us, unavoidable—or at least unavoidable by any text which deals ambitiously with major problems—then what kind of attitude should we adopt towards these texts? Derrida's own tone seems to vary: Husserl, Heidegger, Hegel, and Saussure are treated with more respect than Rousseau and Lévi-Strauss, whose 'blind spots' are noted in a language that is often disparaging. There is always the possibility of stressing an author's blindness, since

the writer writes *in* a language and *in* a logic whose proper system, laws, and life his discourse by definition cannot dominate absolutely. He uses them only by letting himself, after a fashion and up to a point, be governed by the system. And reading must always aim at a certain relationship, unperceived by the writer, between what he commands and what he does not command of the patterns of the language he uses.

(*Of Grammatology*)

One always has the strategic or rhetorical possibility of stressing a writer's blindness to the statement of his text, but since the structures one is revealing are in his text the question of the author's 'awareness' of them is ultimately beside the point. Indeed, Paul de Man has argued persuasively[5] that since Derrida's insights in his reading of Rousseau are all taken from Rousseau's own texts, the claim to be 'correcting' Rousseau's blindness can only be a rhetorical strategy: it makes a good story.

[5] In 'The Rhetoric of Blindness', *Blindness and Insight* (1971).

But if a deconstructive reading does not point out 'errors' in Rousseau, does the same hold for Lévi-Strauss and other contemporary theorists, whose writings also combine critical motifs with metaphysical presuppositions? Derrida's treatment of the writings of structuralism and post-structuralism parallels in many respects his treatment of Saussure. Saussurian structural linguistics first provided the methodological impetus to treat other systems of phenomena as 'languages'—myth, kinship rules, and totemism in Lévi-Strauss, the unconscious in Lacan, the 'grammar' of narrative or of the literary work in Barthes, and the *épistème* of a given historical period as a grammar generating possibilities of discourse in Foucault. Therefore, as one might expect, Derrida finds in structuralism and post-structuralism the same combination of metaphysical presuppositions and critical motifs that his double reading identified in Saussure.

On the one hand, the critical power of these writings has been considerable. The work of Barthes, Lévi-Strauss, Foucault, and Lacan—along, of course, with the texts of Nietzsche, Freud, and Saussure which they use—has stressed difference and systems of differences and has called into question the notion of the self as subject or consciousness which might serve as a source of meaning and a principle of explanation. As Foucault writes, 'The researches of psychoanalysis, of linguistics, of anthropology, have "decentred" the subject in relation to the laws of its desire, the forms of its language, the rules of its actions, or the play of its mythical and imaginative discourse' (*The Archaeology of Knowledge*). To put it very schematically, in each of these fields, arguments citing in some way the priority of difference have made the subject something constituted by or resulting from the play of systems rather than a controlling consciousness which is the master and ultimate origin of systems. Meaning is explained in terms of an underlying system of differences. But the very positing of a system and the attempt at explanation ensure that this critical discourse remains implicated in the metaphysics of presence.

'This necessity is irreducible . . . ,' writes Derrida:

We ought to consider very carefully all its implications. But if nobody can escape this necessity, and if no one is therefore responsible for giving in to it, however little, this does not mean that all the ways of giving in to it are of equal pertinence. The quality and fecundity of a discourse are perhaps measured by the critical rigour with which this relationship to the history of metaphysics and to inherited concepts is thought. . . . It is a question of posing expressly and systematically the problem of the status of a discourse which borrows from a heritage the resources necessary for the deconstruction of that heritage itself.

(Writing and Difference)

Derrida's critique of his four contemporaries bears on their failure to scrutinize with sufficient rigour the status of their own discourse, as Derrida himself is continually doing. He is not asking for an 'awareness' of the problematical nature of their enterprise, for that they have in abundance. They are engaged in a critique of knowledge, truth, objectivity, presence, and at the same time are producing impressive analyses of cultural products and human activities. Their awareness of the problem of their own discourse, which claims knowledge at the same time as it calls knowledge into question, is in a sense beside the point. This awareness, Derrida suggests, should issue in a rigorous questioning of their own categories which will serve to displace those categories. This questioning must leave a track or wake (*sillage*) in the text, as it does in Derrida's own texts, where difference is displaced into *différance*, speech is subsumed under *archi-écriture*, and the *supplément* works its problematical logic.

Lévi-Strauss, Derrida argues, begins with a promising strategy, working within the system he is calling into question, 'conserving in the field of empirical research all those old concepts, while at the same time exposing here and there their limits, treating them as tools which can still be of use', but forgoing claims to truth and identifying his own work as a 'myth of mythology'. But he does not follow through and ask whether all myths of mythology are equivalent. 'If one does not expressly pose this problem one condemns oneself to transforming the supposed transgression of philosophy into an unperceived fault within the domain of philosophy' (ibid.). What is the status of Lévi-Strauss's own myth?

The case of Foucault is even clearer. His histories are a powerful critical force, exposing the conditions of possibility of numerous discursive practices which claim to be grounded in truth, but it is never made clear what relationship his own discourse bears to the *épistème*. After recognizing the problematical nature of his own enterprise, Foucault seems content to plunge ahead into what he calls a 'happy positivism'. Thus, when he writes the history of madness, Foucault exposes the limits of the 'reason' or 'sanity' which has always defined madness, but it is clear, Derrida argues, that Foucault's own enterprise can only be another attempt by reason to define madness and not a project of a different order (ibid.).

In the case of Lacan, whose exploration of the logic of the signifier has affinities with Derrida's own work, the problem is the status of 'truth'. Lacan, says Derrida, claims to reveal the true Freud and presents psychoanalysis as an attempt to discover the truth of the subject or psyche. In Lacan 'truth—cut off from knowledge—is constantly determined as revelation, non-veiling [*non-voilement*], that is to say necessarily as presence, presentation of the present' (*Positions*). The unconscious may be structured like a language, but that language, for Lacan, is controlled, it is not subject to dissemination. In his reading of Poe's 'The Purloined Letter' Lacan argues for order and truth with the lapidary formula, 'a letter always arrives at its destination.' 'It always might not,' answers Derrida in his critique of that reading ('Le Facteur de la vérité').[6] The play of language can never be mastered, though Lacan's unmasterable discourse seems determined to master it.

The case of Roland Barthes is rather different because Barthes himself has abandoned what he once called the 'dream of scientificity' of his early work and, at least since *S/Z*, would deny that his language has any priviledge status or can claim mastery of what it discusses. Derrida has not written explicitly about the position or mode of writing Barthes has adopted (though his discussion of structuralist literary criticism in 'Force et signification' in *Writing and Difference* would apply to Barthes's early work), but he might regret that Barthes had seemingly accepted the distinction between scientific or philosophical discourse on the one hand and literary discourse on the other by shifting his allegiance explicitly from the former to the latter. 'What I want to emphasize', Derrida writes in another connection, 'is that the passage beyond philosophy does not consist in turning the page of philosophy, but in continuing to read philosophers in *a certain way*'

[6] See Barbara Johnson's brilliant discussion in 'The Frame of Reference: Poe, Lacan, Derrida', *Yale French Studies*, nos. 55/6 (1977).

(*Writing and Difference*). A continuing engagement with and deconstruction of philosophical concepts would seem to Derrida a more pertinent and powerful discourse today than an explicit retreat into a literary mode.

Indeed, one of the central issues raised by Derrida's work is that of the relationship between literary and philosophical discourse. One could argue that philosophy has always depended for its existence on a notion of literary discourse and that the move which sets aside certain kinds of language as fictional, rhetorical, in an oblique and problematic relationship to truth, is the gesture by which philosophy, since Plato, has exorcized certain problems and defined itself. This positing of an opposition between the philosophical and the literary has been philosophy's way of recognizing (and containing) the threat which language poses to its activities. It conjures that threat away by positing another realm where language can be as linguistic as it likes and then treating that realm as derivative, problematical, and non-serious. Philosophy has often dreamed of pure logical means of expression which would protect it from the machinations and metaphoricity of words. In treating metaphysics as a discourse befuddled by its own language, as a system of metaphors whose metaphoricity had been forgotten, logical positivists argued that a great deal of philosophy was literary discourse with at best an oblique relation to truth, and by setting aside this sort of language they tried to place themselves within a literal, transparent, non-literary discourse. This stratagem has been repeated in various guises. Even those who called themselves 'ordinary language philosophers' and might have been expected to embrace all language as their province, established their position by setting aside, under the rubric of 'literary' or 'non-serious' language, a great deal of linguistic activity.[7]

This opposition between the literary and the philosophical is another version of the opposition between writing and speech. Certain qualities of language are attributed to writing/literature so that they can be treated as parasitical or derivative and so that the purity and direct relation to thought or truth of speech/philosophy

---

[7] For Derrida's discussion of this move in the work of J. L. Austin, see 'Signature, Event, Context' in *Glyph* (Baltimore, Md.), no. 1 (1977); also in *Marges de la philosophie* (1972).

may be preserved. But speech and philosophy are always tainted, marked by writing/literature. In both cases Derrida's deconstruction reverses the hierarchy by showing that the privileged term can be treated as a special case of the secondary term. Philosophy constituted itself in a direct relation to the Logos by identifying as its Other a fictional and rhetorical mode of discourse, and the demonstration, carried out for example in some of Nietzsche's texts, that philosophy too is a rhetorical structure, based on fictions generated by tropes, leads one to posit what one might call an archi- or proto-literature which would be the common condition of both literature and philosophy. Philosophy cannot escape the rhetorical, the literary, the linguistic. Indeed, Derrida's readings show that so-called philosophical texts are most acute and precise when their figures and their rhetorical strategies are given close attention. Conversely, texts usually identified as literary reveal powerful philosophical deconstructions once the importance of their special logics, like the logic of supplementarity, is recognized.[8]

Derrida's deconstructive reversals are strategic interventions. They do not lay the groundwork for a new discipline—grammatology, he says, is the name of a *question*—but apply pressure to a system of concepts, upset it so as to make its presuppositions and its limits more apparent. Characteristically, Derrida's readings focus on terms which commentators have thought unimportant but which in their double functioning reveal a problematical logic that exceeds and undermines the explicit system of a text. *Supplément, pharmakon, hymen, entame, différance*, and others are undecidable terms, operating in a double register which permits no synthesis and which thus provides leverage for 'undoing' the strategy and presuppositions of the text.

The 'literary' character of Derrida's writing, though flamboyant in a work like *Glas* with its juxtapositions and its exploration of signifying chains, usually derives primarily from the leverage he gains from these signifiers which, like *supplément*, can bring together in a text two meanings which are irreconcilable but which can be made to function together in an argument. The exploitation of the problematical double force that is produced by this play of the

[8] For further discussion see my forthcoming book *The Pursuit of Signs: Semiotics, Literature, Deconstruction.*

signifier enables Derrida to test the limits of logocentrism. What we call a 'literary technique' or a literary moment, when a pun like *différance* produces a conjunction of non-synthesizable meanings, is in fact also a philosophical moment *par excellence*: a breaching of the rationality of logocentrism by inserting, as the lynch-pin of a system, a construct which is not a concept in that it is contradictory.

Derrida's readings combine what we ordinarily think of as the literary play of language with philosophical rigour, not in some mild-mannered compromise but in their most radical forms. What gives Derrida's writings their special power is this combination: he argues within a particular philosophical system but at the same time attempts through the productivity of language to breach or exceed that system. 'Deconstructing philosophy', he writes,

is thus a matter of working through the structured genealogy of its concepts in the most scrupulous fashion, from within, but at the same time from a certain external perspective which it cannot name or describe, and of determining what this history may have concealed or forbidden, emerging as history from this repression in which it has some stake. At this point, through this movement, both faithful and violent, back and forth between the inside and the outside of philosophy—[the philosophy] that is to say of the West—there results a certain textual activity and product [*travail textuel*] which gives great pleasure.

(*Positions*)

Great pleasure to all those who have the interest and patience to follow the argument of texts which displace or undo the most fundamental categories of our intellectual life.

Bibliography

Jacques Derrida was born near Algiers, in what was then French Algeria, in 1930. He was educated at the École Normale Supérieure in Paris, and now teaches the History of Philosophy there.

BOOKS
L'Écriture et la différence (Paris, 1967); English translation, *Writing and Difference* (Chicago, 1978)

La Voix et la phénomène (Paris, 1967); English translation, *Speech and Phenomena* (Evanston, Ill., 1973)

De la grammatologie (Paris, 1967); English translation, *Of Grammatology* (Baltimore, Md., and London, 1977)

La Dissémination (Paris, 1972)

Marges de la philosophie (Paris, 1972). English translations of certain essays from this collection have appeared in various places. There has been no complete translation.

Positions (Paris, 1972). An English translation of the title interview in this volume appeared in *Diacritics*, vol. II, no. 4 and vol. III, no. 1.

L'Archéologie de la frivole (Paris, 1976). The introduction to an edition of Condillac's *Essai sur l'origine de la connaissance humaine* published in 1973.

Glas (Paris, 1974)

Éperons. Les styles de Nietzsche (Venice, 1976). Includes translation in English. Subsequently also published in Paris in a French edition.

La Vérité en peinture (Paris, 1978)

TRANSLATION

Edmund Husserl, *L'Origine de la géométrie*, translated with an introduction by Derrida (Paris, 1962); English translation, *Edmund Husserl's 'Origin of Geometry'* (Stony Brook, N.Y., 1978)

There are valuable discussions of Derrida in English by Gayatri Spivak with her translation of *Of Grammatology* (see above); by Paul de Man in *Blindness and Insight* (New York, 1971); and by Richard Rorty, 'Philosophy as a Kind of Writing', in *New Literary History*, Autumn 1978.

Index